A CULINARY TOUR
Through

ALABAMA
HISTORY

A CULINARY TOUR

Through

ALABAMA
HISTORY

—— ◗ ——

MONICA TAPPER

AMERICAN PALATE

Published by American Palate
A Division of The History Press
Charleston, SC
www.historypress.com

Illustrations by Raphael Barrington.

First published 2021

Manufactured in the United States

ISBN 9781467149730

Library of Congress Control Number: 2021943422

For my grandmother Marilyn Mertle Blaine, who taught me that banana splits are healthy—the ice cream has calcium, the cherries and bananas are fruit, and the pecans have protein.

CONTENTS

ACKNOWLEDGEMENTS

Thank you to The History Press and especially Joe Gartrell for all of their help and for keeping me calm over the past few months. This book was a group effort. Carol Cleaver and Blake Denton worked for hours, editing different parts of this book. Mary Collette Hamner and her daughters Titania Collette and Abigail Hamner cooked every recipe here—and even a few that did not make it into the final version of the book. Lesley Hicks traveled around and kept me company while I drove through Alabama. Chris Burroughs (despite his terrible taste in music), Kathy Shannon, Kouri Allen, Sarah McLeod, Nick Beeson, Jada Jones, and Mike Venton are my graduate school crew, and I'm forever grateful to know them. All of the gorgeous illustrations and the map included in this book were drawn by graphic artist Raphael Barrington.

I am grateful to so many historians, chefs, and others in Alabama who took the time to help me, including Meredith McDonough from the Alabama Department of Archives and History; Jen Knutson from the Center for Archaeological Studies at the University of South Alabama; Susan Stein and Michael Herzog from the Grand Hotel; Ninon Parker from Belle Mont Mansion; Mayor Nikki Sprader and Lyla Peebles of Mooresville; Andrew and Diane Moore from the Columbiana Inn; and Stan Reynolds from Galley and Garden. An extra big thank-you to Kim French from One Fine Day Photography who took the time to do a wonderful photoshoot. Thank you to Gary Mullen, Elizabeth Bates, Greg Schmidt and Tommy Brown at Auburn University for their help with the Gosse illustration, and of course, thank you to Jonathon Vines and the British Library for permission to use the image here. And, as always, a big thank-you to the Bragg ladies: Lynn Stewart, Trattie Ollis, Irene Dietrich, and Katie Mulkerne. These ladies are always supportive of whatever project I'm working on, but they also taught me the value of a tea party.

There are also people who took time out of their busy schedules to help, and I am incredibly grateful for them. Without them, this book could not have been written. John Sledge from the Mobile Historic Development Commission showed me how to get this project off the ground. Not only did Ricia Hendrick from Elevator World translate my contract from legalese to English, but she has also always been the adult in the room for me. Cart Blackwell from the Mobile Carnival Museum taught me how to conduct research. Christopher Maloney, Melinda Farr Brown, and Mitchell Brown helped me understand the magnificent suffragist Bossie O'Brien. Tony May and his aunt Zelda taught me about the lives of Kenny May and Clyde May. And of course, thank you to Holly Day, Melanie Thornton, Lara Lander, and Danielle Vertrees for helping me out with locations! Thanks also to Paula Webb for helping me through this whole process.

Thanks to the University of South Alabama for my education—in particular, my thesis advisors, Dr. Marsha Hamilton, Dr. Martha Jane Brazy, and Dr. Gregory Waselkov. Other professors who helped me along the way were Dr. Victoria L. Rivizzigno, Dr. Susan McCready, and Dr. Mir Zohair Husain. And of course, thank you to my other family at Wallace Community College in Selma. Felicia Sanders, Monique Ford, Dr. Tara White, Ghytana Goings, and Michael Walker are the best team of people anyone could work with, and I am grateful every day for them. And of course, thank you to my students—I appreciate all your hard work and dedication.

Nothing is done without family. Not only did my sister Sarah Tapper Roberts read parts of the book, but she and my brother-in-law Jared gave me the cutest nephew, Cameron Roberts. It was touch and go there for a while, but it turns out Cameron really does love cake. My grandmother Marilyn Blaine is the best grandma in the world, and her mother, Florence Mertle, was clearly the strongest woman who ever lived. Finally, a big thank-you to my husband, Dewan Rahman, and all of my extended family in Bangladesh. I finally found a family who cooks with flavor. If you ever asked the Rahman family if one could cook with too many peppers, they would not answer you; they would just quietly add more peppers.

INTRODUCTION

Our ancestors left us a guidebook to not only see how they lived but to taste it. In the case of Marion, a small town in Dallas County, the townspeople left us a two-hundred-year-old party. Marion was founded in 1817, two years before Alabama became a state. It grew quickly, even though much of Alabama was still frontier land. By 1827, the little town had already built their second jail, a small school, and a few small shops.[1] The largest, most elaborate social event in Marion's ten years was the housewarming party thrown by William Barron in 1827 to celebrate his new house, which was the first frame house built in the town. There were at least twenty-five people there for the party, which started off with a stag dance, or a dance in which only the young men were allowed to dance.[2]

Apparently, the young men of Marion were not terribly graceful, as they were described as having "not much regard for steps—every man for himself." A local violinist brought his famous violin, known to everyone there as "Pine Bark," and played the popular tune "Miss McLeod," and a fiddler played "Billy in the Low Ground" for the guests to dance to.[3] Both songs can be heard online. "Miss McLeod" has a bit of Irish sound to it, but "Billy in the Low Ground" cannot really be labeled as anything other than bluegrass gone wild. One can only imagine those arms and legs flailing about.

While the young men danced, the guests in the next room were working on the more serious business of stirring five gallons of eggnog. As they stirred and beat the eggs, they kept time to the fiddler by tapping with quill pens and spoons. The recipe they used probably looked something like the recipe for eggnog from *The Gulf City Cook Book*, by the Ladies of the St. Francis Street Methodist Episcopal Church in Mobile, Alabama, from 1878:

> *To each egg, allow one small wine glass of brandy, one tablespoonful of sugar; beat the whites and yolks separately. After beating the yolks well, gradually add the sugar, then the brandy; also allow about three wine glasses of rum to about one dozen eggs; pour in the milk, as much as you like—say a quart to a dozen eggs—and last, stir in the whites when they are as light as they can be beaten.*[4]

"Every man to his glass," called the master of ceremonies when the eggnog was ready. The dancing stopped just long enough for every guest to drink several glasses, each serving saturated with copious amounts of cognac. After the initial drinks, the real party began. The dancing resumed, only then, everyone was on the dance floor. In addition to the eggnog, there was wine, whiskey, and brandy, although the existent food was only recorded as "the tables were filled with every procurable luxury."[5] What those luxury items consisted of in a town with only one frame house and enough liquor to sink a boat on the Alabama River, we will never know. The townspeople of Marion partied until dawn.

You can hear the music, imagine the funny young men dancing, and taste the eggnog. It's a magical image, but let's not stop there. Let's get in the car and drive to Mobile. There is some tea you should drink at the Bragg-Mitchell Mansion.

Alfred and Minnie Mitchell were the last private owners of the mansion. Minnie bought the house for $20,000 in the 1930s and spent the following three decades carefully tending her home. She spent hours and hours just taking down and putting up curtains according to the seasons' demands. The house was decorated with antiques that Minnie purchased on her trips to New Orleans, many of which are still there today. She planted azaleas, trees, and flowers and spent many hours in her gardens. She also threw parties, although her parties were a lot less exciting than the throwdown party in Marion. There were bridge parties in the bridge room, where the ladies did a bit of gambling. Minnie also threw tea parties, and today, the mansion still does. Twice a year, the Bragg-Mitchell Mansion throws open its doors and welcomes tourists to sit on Minnie's couches and drink tea brewed by Alabama ladies. The mansion can be found at the bottom of the map included in this book.

Map of Alabama History: each location on the tour serves up delicious food. Read about each one in these chapters. Each location can be found on the following pages:

MEMORIES OF FOOD

Food memoirs written by Ruth Reichl, M.F.K. Fischer, Kwame Onwuachi, and others reveal their lives through food memories. Their work is powerful, but if we can feel and taste their memories, we can certainly do the same with those of the people who left records of life in Alabama. This book will try to capture the lives of regular people, not celebrities, who lived through different eras in Alabama. They have left us their remembrances of life and flavors through diaries, letters, and even newspapers. Because of length and record limitations, we can only view fragments, but these moments are enough to give us a window into another era.

Another way to connect to the people who came before us is to eat a meal in a historical setting. This book contains several locations that offer food but were not built as restaurants. That was the only rule I followed when writing this book; every location had to be historically significant but not as a restaurant. In these pages, there are homes, hotels, shops, and even a monastery where you can go and eat. Sometimes, you will be able to eat a whole meal; other times, you can only buy a condiment or some chocolate.

This is not meant to be a full history of Alabama—that is a much longer series of books. It's not meant to be a food history; I'll leave that to the food historians. It's not meant to be a cookbook. After a few fires and several plates of raw food, my husband asked me not to cook anymore. This is meant to be a snapshot of the lives of people from the past, using the physical connection of food. It's a meaningful way to eat, travel, and taste what Alabama has cooking on the stove. If this idea makes you hungry, turn the page.

1
EAT YOUR HISTORY

In the Beginning

The first question people from Alabama will always ask you is, "Where are your people from?" I could not even qualify as a southerner, much less as an Alabamian, because my mother was from California, and my father was from Holland. They were hippies who met in the late 1960s on a kibbutz in Israel, where my mother picked apples, and my father was a shepherd. They ran around the Middle East and Europe for a while, sometimes working, though occasionally homeless, but eventually, they made their way to America. Before heading to California, my parents' plan was to visit my grandparents in Alabama because my grandfather had finally fulfilled his dream of owning land "down south" with his own vineyard and orchard. But that old hippie spirit had not completely died out yet, and they ran out of money once they made it to Alabama. This financial oversight is why my sister and I were born and raised in Alabama instead of California with our cousins.

My sister and I knew we were not like the other kids. Neither of us had ever heard of grits until we started going to sleepovers. We did not drink sweet tea in our house, and we were seriously confused about our friends and their unreasonable overuse of ice cubes in their drinks. We hardly ever ate seafood, and we definitely never ate any deer meat in our house. My mother had apparently never walked down the spice aisle at the grocery store and was terrified of salt. Just like tourists, my sister and I learned about Alabama foods through native Alabamians—those Alabamians whose people were from Alabama. Generous southern mothers fed us homemade biscuits and butter, grits with oh-so-wonderful salt, and home-brewed sweet tea.

Along with my southern food education, there was still the orchard and vineyard left behind by my grandfather, who had planted native Alabama crops. Today, there is not much left of it aside from some overgrown weeds, but twenty years ago, there were thick, fat muscadines and scuppernongs. My grandfather made wine from his grapes, and my grandmother canned the pears and persimmons that grew wild in the orchard. The grandchildren ate pecans off the ground before much else could be done with them.

Because I discovered the food of Alabama in a very different way than the people I grew up with, I am both a native Alabamian and a tourist. Therefore, seeing one's identity through food is something I take very seriously. I am a southerner, an Alabamian; I drink my tea sweetened; and I eat my tomatoes fried. I also know that even Yankees can feel southern if given the right tools.

Of course, food in Alabama has changed quite a bit since the state's founding in 1819. For one thing, Alabamians don't cook over open fires anymore. Kitchens are inside our homes. Does food cooked over a fire taste different than food cooked on a stovetop? Anyone who has grilled in their backyard knows the answer to this. But appliances are not the only reason our food tastes different. Our food is bought from the grocery store—it comes in boxes and bags. Many hands come into contact with our food before we ever cook it. Green beans are planted, grown, harvested, packed, and shipped by strangers long before they arrive at the grocery store. The days of picking a mess of green beans in the field and slaughtering chickens on the porch are over. And although this is necessary for our modern life, it does change the flavor of our foods. Any chef will tell you that the secret to delicious food is freshness.

Freshness extends past the green beans and chicken. Cornbread and hominy were made from fresh corn by Alabama pioneers. Eventually, wheat was grown, harvested, milled, and made into bread. Today, corn and wheat are usually heavily processed, and by the time it hits our kitchen tables, it will look nothing like what it did two hundred years ago. Typically, large bread companies mix several kinds of wheat together to make the bread that winds up on the bakery aisle of the grocery store. But there are those diligent artisans who have found ways to reproduce heirloom grains. A few companies like Anson Mills provide flours, grits, and rice from heirloom grains, which are passed from one generation to the next.[6] That old French

Fireplace in a kitchen, west side of the slave house, Cunningham Plantation. Cherokee, Colbert County, Alabama. *Courtesy of the Library of Congress.*

Fireplace in a kitchen. Leighton, Colbert County, Alabama. *Courtesy of the Library of Congress.*

term *terroir*, usually associated with stuffy wine drinkers, applies to bread as well. The same grain growing in different regions will make bread taste completely different.[7]

Scott Peacock is an award-winning chef, writer, and grain artisan from Hartford, Alabama. After several years working as a famous chef in Atlanta, he returned to Alabama and bought Reverie, a historic home in Marion, Alabama. In this antebellum home, which still retains its marks in the attic from Union occupation during the Civil War, Peacock has renovated the kitchen in order to give baking lessons. Peacock grows his own heirloom grain, purple straw, on the property. He then shows guests how to make biscuits from heirloom wheat in an antebellum house, built in 1858.[8] It doesn't get more authentic than that.

How can food connect us to our history when modern fare is so different? Not everything has changed. Sometimes, place and tradition are enough. There are also those industrious artisans and chefs like Scott Peacock, who use original ingredients and prepare them in original ways, just as our ancestors did. However, this book is about eating, not cooking. There are enough books about cooking our ancestral foods, but until now, there has been no celebration of eating that food. California cuisine, new American cuisine, farm-to-table—all the major movements in American food history are chef-driven, so chefs get the glory. American chefs and writers like James Beard, Julia Child, and Craig Claiborne have shaped our collective palate and how we think about food. Beard was a pioneer in the food industry and one of the first "celebrity" American chefs. Child made complex French cooking accessible to Americans for the first time.[9] But these chefs were from the West Coast. Claiborne was a Mississippi boy who grew up in the delta and reinvented (or invented) the food critic's job. Thomas McNamee opens his wonderful biography of Claiborne with the southerner's grievances about American restaurants, which had been printed on the front page of the *New York Times* in 1959: "Elegance of Cuisine Is on Wane in the U.S."[10] You know things were about to get hairy after that.

The history of American cuisine is important to study, as is food history itself. But the people who eat the food are usually forgotten in the pages of food history, even though eating a meal can be full of intricate nuances. The image of a person eating alone in their own kitchen, with the TV on in the background, evokes a much different feeling than the same person eating with other people at a restaurant, laughing, and sharing stories. Food is universal. Bitter, sweet, sour—these are flavors we all understand, no matter what era we live through. There are aspects of history that can be difficult

Craig Claiborne, a Mississippi boy who became the food editor and restaurant critic for the *New York Times. Courtesy of the Library of Congress.*

for us to understand through our modern lens, but the flavor of food is where all those barriers break down and allow us to connect with history.

When we eat the same foods as people of the past, we carry on their traditions. When we eat a meal in a historical building, we share the same physical space with those people from the past. When we do so with the understanding that the place is historically significant, it ties us to the people who came before us. It's by connecting with the people who ate the food that we can have a better understanding of life in long-ago Alabama. The foods they ate, who they shared them with, the conversations they had—this is how we can have a window into their world.

TOWARD ALABAMA

Alabama became a state in 1819, but there were people living, laughing, and eating there long before Alabama was admitted into the Union. Natives had lived in Alabama for centuries before the White migrants came to settle the land. They were usually from South Carolina, North Carolina, Georgia, and Tennessee, although there were more than a few New Englanders who made their way to Alabama, looking for better opportunities than those they had in the North. Much of Alabama was wild frontier land with hardly any infrastructure in the early 1800s, and whatever life the settlers found for themselves had to be earned through blood and sweat.

New immigrants to Alabama during the pioneer days shared one trait with all new pioneers in America: a love/hate relationship with wheat and corn. Wheat was what the original pioneers had known back home in England, and from America's earliest days, wheat was associated with proper English food. This idea was firmly entrenched in the New World, even though wheat did not grow nearly as well as corn here. Eventually, wheat bread became prevalent in America, but it never completely replaced corn, the native crop.[11]

Corn may have been the crop that was needed to survive, but it still had to be grown. The time between settling the land and harvesting the first crop of corn was difficult. The first settlers in Madison County lived on venison jerk until the first crop of corn could be harvested. After the first ears of corn had been reaped, the settlers ate hominy, but they also ate cornbread, which they made from a rude mortar and pestle, as there was not yet a mill to grind the corn.[12]

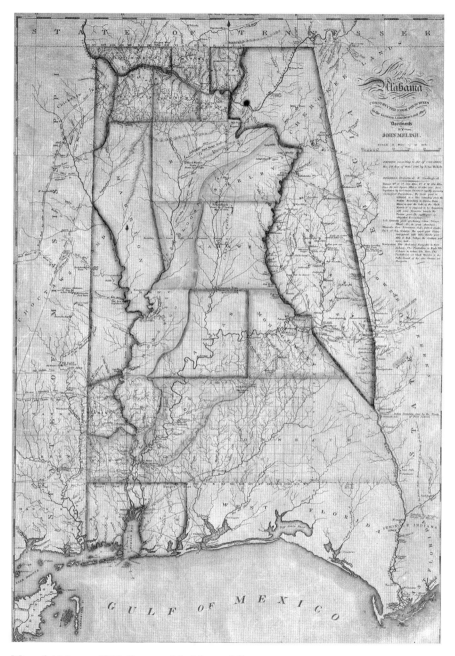

Map of Alabama, 1819. *Courtesy of the Library of Congress.*

Mrs. Brown in her smokehouse with home-canned goods and cured meat. Prairie Farms, Alabama. *Courtesy of the Library of Congress.*

New settlers also found natural sweetener from the honey in beehives and salt from salt springs. Access to salt was important, as it allowed the settlers to preserve meat. If salt springs were not available, the meat could be smoked, which would also have preserved it for the long winters when food was scarce. In Alabama's forests, settlers had access to wild game, such as deer, bear, fox, wolf, beaver, panther, and even wildcat. Of course, there were also wild pigeons, turkeys, ducks, and geese. For the truly desperate, there were wild squirrels.[13]

Food is only part of the story of Alabama. There are many historic homes in the South that offer educational tours, and these provide people a view into history that cannot be gained by simply reading a book. But a tour is a passive way to appreciate history. Eating is not passive; it's an active way to be a part of history. Eating is the difference between passive appreciation and active participation. Taking part in history—reliving tradition, not just viewing it—is how you connect with it. Eat your history; it's delicious.

2
ALABAMA BECOMES A STATE

1819—1820s

ANNE ROYALL

Anne Newport Royall was one of Alabama's most famous early tourists. She was not a typical woman of the era and did not behave in the way that women were supposed to. Never one to be demure or quiet, Anne had grievances, and she shared them—publicly. She traveled the country and wrote books about her experiences. If someone treated her badly, she wrote about it. On the other hand, if someone treated her well, she wrote about that, too. People flinched when they heard she was coming. At times, they could be downright hostile. An innkeeper once broke her leg when he pushed her down a flight of stairs after stating her business was not wanted.[14]

Born in Maryland in 1769 and raised in a log cabin on the frontier, Anne grew up a bit rough around the edges. At the age of sixteen, she met Captain William Royall after she and her mother made a desperate and poverty-stricken trek to Virginia, where he offered his own home as shelter for the two women. They were married in 1797, and it seems to have been a happy marriage. He died in 1812, leaving the bulk of his large estate to Anne, but he left out all other potential heirs with the last name of Royall. This did not sit well with the family, and by 1819, the Royalls managed to overturn the will, rendering Anne penniless at the age of fifty.[15] To make money, she became a travel writer and visited West Virginia, Alabama, Tennessee, Virginia, Washington, Delaware, New York, Pennsylvania, Illinois, Indiana, and Ohio. Travel was difficult, as roads were in terrible condition, and stagecoaches were not remotely reliable. There was no AAA to fix a broken carriage, so sometimes, Anne would have to walk for miles.

Anne's claim to notoriety occurred in 1829, in Washington, D.C., where she had made an enemy of her neighbors, the Presbyterian Church. Though Anne was a Christian, she had no patience for organized religion. She and the members of the church had never gotten on well, but in June 1829, the church made repeated and very unwelcome attempts to convert her. In addition to praying outside her window, the boys threw rocks and shouted at her when she came into the street. The church became so frustrated with their failed attempts to save her soul, that they filed legal charges against her. She was accused of being a public nuisance, a brawler, and a common scold, which is an archaic term for a nagging, difficult woman. Only the last charge stuck, and she went on trial and was convicted. She was sentenced to be ducked in the Potomac River. A device for the ducking was built for her punishment, but in the end, the sentence was commuted to a fine of ten dollars, plus court costs. Among her other achievements, Anne is the only person in American history to be convicted for being a scold.[16]

A decade before Anne's famous trial, and five years before she went broke, she traveled in style to visit Alabama, one of her favorite vacation spots. In January 1818, she traveled for three days from Huntsville to Melton's Bluff, a distance of either forty-five or seventy miles, depending on where you cross the Tennessee River. Melton's Bluff is at the head of Muscle Shoals and was named for John Melton, a pirate who got rich from robbing ships that were traveling down the Tennessee River. After murdering the crews, Melton would steal their enslaved people and any booty on the ship. He built a large plantation and bought an enslaved person who was trained as a first-rate chef from Baltimore. His parties were legendary, and even when Anne arrived two years after Melton's death, she heard stories of the best liquors, meats, and coffee being served at his house. Unfortunately for his Native wife, who was not allowed to cook, Melton had not given up his violent ways, even after he retired from piracy. On the rare occasions when she attempted to cook any of her beloved Native dishes, her husband took his horsewhip to her back, and the enslaved chef would return to the kitchen.[17]

During Anne's stay in Melton's Bluff, it was a budding place, with three shops, a pharmacy, a hatter, two doctors, several mechanics, and more than a few taverns. Anne boarded with the Pettis family. The household included Colonel Pettis, a large, happy man originally from Virginia; his young, beautiful wife with sparkling black eyes; and their two sons. The wife's two sisters, one widow and her child, and the barkeeper also lived in the house while Anne boarded with them.[18] (The following breakfast meal was recorded by Anne herself but has been shortened and edited for clarity.)

On February 19, a badly dressed villager stopped by during breakfast. After shaking hands all around, the colonel told his wife to bring another plate, knife, and fork so their guest could join.

"Come, sir, take a dram first," the colonel said, and then to his wife, "Hand a glass, Maria."

After the villager took a drink, the colonel asked, "How is your family, sir?"

"Why, I'm obliged to you, colonel, they're all about, but Mary: she's got her ague yet. How's it with yourself?"

The colonel answered, "We are all well thank you, sir. Let me help you to another piece of steak. Have some of the gravy, sir. Well, let's hear the news: who do the people talk of voting for?" And then, "Take some butter, sir."

"Well, some of them is mighty scared of losing their land, and some of them has a mind to stand them a pull. I tell you what, colonel, it's hard upon a poor man, after all, after clearing himself a smart patch of ground and putting it under a good fence, see, and building him a snug cabin, and then for a rich man like you, colonel, because he rebounds in most money, to come to buy it from over his head, see tell you what, it's a little sort of hard. But I reviewed it from the first. I saw how it was going and sold out."

Maria poured more coffee.

The colonel asked, "Well, but tell me, old fellow, who do the people talk of voting for on Flint?"

"Why, to tell the truth, colonel, they're pretty much divided. Some of them talks of running Dr. Crab."

Maria set the decanter down on the table.

"Some of them talk of voting for Lawyer L."

"Take some whiskey, sir," the colonel told him. "But tell me, who do you intend to vote for?"

"Well, I was just going to say, I don't hold with sending none of these here doctors, and lawyers, and philosophers. I look upon it, see, that there here men of learning just lay their heads together and just make laws to oppress the poor. I'm for supporting a plain farmer, like myself, colonel, that will act upon economical principles, ain't I right?"

"But tell us, old fellow, have you any corn to sell up your way?"

"Why it's pretty tolerable scarce. I raised a fine chance this year, and my wife had the finest passel of truck, I dare say, she had greens enough

to supply the whole neighborhood, but Jim Wilson's critters broke in and almost destroyed the whole affair, so it is, I shall have to buy."

The villager brought the conversation back to politics and invited Colonel Pettis to Dr. Crab's barbeque, where the doctor planned to make a stump speech, and there were already two barrels of whiskey ordered for the event. The political barbeque was a popular social event during election season, where men gathered for barbeque, and there would be lots of shoat and whiskey. A few years after this breakfast, Alabamians of the urban variety campaigned to end these rowdy events. However, no amount of campaigning could end whisky drinking during election season, and even without the barbeque, there was still a lot of whiskey given out by politicians running for office. It was not seen as bribery; whiskey was just a way of life, and everyone drank a lot of it.[19]

After the invitation to barbeque and whiskey, the other ladies left the room, but Anne remained to listen to the conversation. She thought it an interesting aspect of human nature that the more educated and polished a man becomes, the more he is able to conceal himself. She still could not tell which candidate Colonel Pettis preferred, but the villager had given himself away, and she was happy to see his honesty shine through. He invited the colonel to his house to go hunting when another villager came to the door. The third gentleman received his own steak and hot coffee. The men discussed the price of corn, gossiped about men around town, raccoons, politics, and then over more whiskey, settled the affairs of the nation.

Melton's Bluff was renamed Marathon when Alabama became a state, but it is presently an abandoned town in Lawrence County. Today, there is a marker to commemorate Melton's Bluff as seen and recorded by Anne.

Years later, when Anne was broke and writing travel books to pay the bills, she returned to Alabama. She and many other travel writers journeyed over the old routes, which stretched from Fort Mitchell to Mobile, that were first left by Natives and then by Andrew Jackson during the Creek Indian War. It took several days for a wagon to reach the other end of the road, and as usual, whether or not the taverns and inns had wheat bread or cornbread was always noted.[20]

James Stuart, a Scottish traveler, stayed in Harris's Hotel near Fort Bainbridge in March 1830. He was sadly without any wheat bread for dinner, but there was "coffee, tea, venison, fowls, ham, eggs, etc." At the next hotel on the route, he ate "chicken pie, ham, vegetables, pudding, and pie." Also, for dessert, there was "dried fruits, preserved strawberries, and plums." He liked everything, but he especially liked the preserved plum and was pleased to note there was wine and brandy.[21]

Thomas Hamilton, another Scottish traveler, in April 1831, stopped in a Native tavern on the way to Fort Mitchell. There was no bread there at all, but for supper, he ate eggs, broiled venison, and cakes made from fried corn. The following day, his group stopped at a Native cottage, where he ate eggs, venison, and corn, which he was happy to get. On the third day, they stopped at an inn kept by an American with three unattractive Native wives, who served an equally unattractive breakfast of bad coffee, rancid venison, and corn cakes.[22]

In addition to bread or the lack of it, travelers generally enjoyed milk punch along the route. The basic recipe for those traveling the untamed roads was: milk with sugar, rum, and a bit of nutmeg.[23] This is still a popular drink today, but as always, modern people have spiced it up with additional ingredients, like vanilla, cream, and even orange juice. To properly enjoy the drink like our ancestors did, keep it to the four basic ingredients.

Ebenezer Hearn

New migrants to the state of Alabama were focused on survival. Luxuries and comforts, both physical and spiritual, had to take second place to survival. Traveling preachers filled the spiritual void, and by 1819, there were eleven itinerant preachers in the state. One of these eleven preachers was Ebenezer Hearn, who was sent to Alabama by the Flint River Conference of Nashville in 1818 to preach and organize churches. He would eventually become Methodism's best-known circuit rider, as his circuit included up to twenty different churches. Originally from North Carolina, he moved to Tennessee as a child. He became licensed to preach in 1815, and in 1816, he joined the Tennessee Conference, which served North Alabama.[24]

Ebenezer was already familiar with the area, as he had fought in the Creek Indian War under Andrew Jackson. In 1813, the war began as a civil war between the Creeks, but by the time Ebenezer had volunteered for battle in 1814, it was a large-scale war between the Lower Creeks (Red Sticks), the Upper Creeks (White Sticks), and their American allies, although none of the three groups were homogenous. After some brutal battles and a few massacres, the war ended with the Treaty of Fort Jackson after the Battle of Horseshoe Bend. This treaty effectively forced most of the Creeks off their land and opened up 23 million acres of land in Alabama for White settlers.[25] When Ebenezer was sent into this area for preaching in 1818, he knew what to expect. During the war, he had witnessed forced marches through the territory that would soon become the state of Alabama, fierce battles, and starvation. During one month in particular, Ebenezer was forced to eat acorns, nuts, herbs, and dry cowhide to keep from starving. But he was determined to stay alive, because even while he starved and heard the cries of the dying soldiers, he felt a deep inner tug to one day serve God. This pushed him to keep going in his darker moments.[26]

Ebenezer Hearn. *Courtesy of the Alabama Department of Archives and History.*

Ebenezer's very first sermon in Alabama was preached at Bear Meat Cabin, an area named for the home of a Creek chief that had become a stopping place for travelers by the time Ebenezer had arrived there. Today, the area that was known as Bear Meat Cabin is the town of Blountsville. From Bear Meat Cabin, Ebenezer went to present-day Birmingham, Jones Valley, Roupe's Valley, Hill Settlement, and present-day Centerville, and then he went to Wilson's Hill, which is now called Montevallo.[27]

In 1822, he married Mary Walker, and the couple had at least five children. In 1837, the Hearn family moved into a federal-style home in the area that is now Camden, Wilcox County. Even though we don't know for certain when the house was built, it's safe to assume that it predates the Greek Revival madness that swept through the South a few decades later. This home would be referred to as the Hearn Place until 1898, when the Gaines family bought it. In 1985, two descendants of the Gaines family, Betty Gaines Kennedy and Hayden Gaines Marsh, opened the Gaines Ridge Dinner Club inside their family home.[28] Today, supper can be eaten at the home of Ebenezer Hearn from Thursday to Saturday between 5:30 p.m. and 9:00 p.m. In March 2020, my friend Lesley and I set out to eat dinner at Ebenezer's house.

Gaines Ridge Dinner Club
933 Highway 10 East
Camden, Alabama 36726

Serves dinner Thursday through Saturday
5:30 p.m.–9:00 p.m. | 334-682-9707

Originally from Missouri, Lesley has lived in Alabama for the past twenty years or so, but that old idea that you must be born in a place to be from there is true in Lesley's case. She does love fried foods, but in all of our years of friendship, I've never seen her order a sweet tea. For an Alabamian, that's just not natural. We left from Mobile, and it took us almost three hours to get to Ebenezer's house. But then again, I am a slow driver, and the average traveler may not need as much time. We chose to take the interstate most of the way there, but when we got on the highway near Atmore in Escambia County, we passed through what is left of the Creek Territory. Ebenezer might not have thought it was as ironic as we did that in order to eat dinner at his home, we had to pass through the territory that, today, belongs to the last remaining descendants of the Creek Indian War, the Poarch Band of Creek Indians. They are the only federally recognized tribe in the state of Alabama. Their sole casino (which is impossible to miss) is the only skyscraper for hundreds of miles. It is, in fact, possible to eat at the buffet in the casino, but neither the food nor the skyscraper is historic.

We arrived at Ebenezer's house at 5:30 p.m., just in time for our reservation. From the parking area in front of the house, a few outbuildings are still visible, but whether or not they are original to the property is anyone's guess. When we went in through the original entrance, we walked right into one of the original four rooms in the downstairs portion of Ebenezer's house. There is also one original bedroom upstairs, and the other rooms were added in the 1990s. This was a relief to us because we had wondered on the ride over how a circuit rider could have purchased such a large home, but the fact that most of it is additional space made more sense.

We were seated in one of the original rooms and greeted by not only our server but the family as well. Sweeping through the rooms carrying bread baskets or seating guests and chatting with regulars, the family is certainly the beating heart of the restaurant. When we asked if we could see the rest of the home, the family was very gracious and gave us a little tour. After talking with them for a while, we learned that our sweet hostess was Ms. Betty's daughter-in-law. Ms. Betty retired at the age of eighty-four, and her daughter-in-law and family now run the restaurant. Although exhausted, our hostess clearly enjoyed what she was doing, and her joy, along with carrying on the family tradition, made the entire atmosphere feel very relaxed.

We ate dinner in the front-left dining room, one of the original rooms, which meant that, at one time, Ebenezer and his family had been in the same room. The fireplace and mantel look to be original, but the furniture and knickknacks are not. This is how it should be, since the public is generally not supposed to use authentic artifacts. It is enough to sit in the same space as Ebenezer—to imagine him there with his family, warming his hands by the fire or possibly preparing his sermons over a pint of ale. In this same room, we ate fried green tomatoes that tasted of the salty blue-green hidden parts of the ocean, but they were softly crisp and lush. The menu is full of modern southern fare: steaks, seafood, hush puppies—more suited to meat eaters than to vegetarians. After a meal of shrimp and crabmeat casserole, baked potatoes, salad, and rolls, we ordered the famous black bottom pie for dessert. This pie was gargantuan, and neither of us could finish our half of the piece of pie. We left happy, full of good southern food and ready for the trip back. It was well worth the drive, and we left Ebenezer's house in good spirits.

3

EARLY STATEHOOD

1820s–1830s

Belle Mont Mansion
1569 Cook Lane
Tuscumbia, Alabama 35674

Sells honey during the summer (while supplies last).
During the last week of June, lunch is served on the courtyard
during the "Art of the Dish" exhibit.
256-381-5052

The first settlers in Alabama would have been overjoyed at finding beehives, because honey might have been their only source of sweetener. Honey is still a natural resource in Alabama. At the Belle Mont Mansion in Tuscumbia, the historic home sells jars of honey made from bees on the property during the summer months. As the bees are buzzing about, stealing pollen from flowers that are grown on the property, the taste of their honey is made by incorporating the land itself. Whereas bees who use pollen from lavender flowers produce honey that tastes like lavender, these bees produce honey that tastes like Alabama history.[29]

Belle Mont was built for Dr. Alexander Williams Mitchell in the late 1820s. Born in Virginia, Dr. Mitchell graduated from the University of Edinburgh in Scotland before settling in Tuscumbia in 1820. In Alabama, he enjoyed professional success as a doctor, planter, and politician, though his private life was tumultuous. His sixteen-year-old daughter, Isabella, died in December 1825, less than a year after her marriage to James Elliot, a Scottish immigrant.[30] His wife, Eliza, died in August 1823, and he was remarried that October to Joanna. His second wife was a city girl from Philadelphia who did not care for northern Alabama, as she thought it was "a lonely, forsaken land."[31]

Belle Mont was built in the Palladian style, a style influenced by Italian Renaissance architect Andrea Palladio. The name Belle Mont means "lovely mountain," and as one of the features of Palladian architecture is incorporating a hilltop into a building, this name is fitting.[32] However, it's tempting to think the name might also be a nod to Dr. Mitchell's daughter Isabella, who died right before the house was built.[33] Thomas Jefferson designed his house and the University of Virginia in the same Palladian style, and it has been suggested that someone familiar with Jefferson's

Belle Mont Mansion in Tuscumbia. *Courtesy of the Library of Congress.*

designs had a hand in designing Belle Mont, as there are many similarities between the two homes.[34]

At his new home, Dr. Mitchell grew cotton and corn and owned 152 enslaved people, some of whom did the actual construction of Belle Mont. But Dr. Mitchell did not stay for long. In 1833, he sold the property to Isaac and Catherine Winston. Today, the house is owned by the Alabama Historical Commission and is open to the public for historical tours and events.[35] Belle Mont Mansion hosts an annual event during the last week of June called "The Art of the Dish," which includes an exhibit of antique china and a box lunch meal served on the courtyard.

In the fall of 2020, the wonderful museum director Ninon Parker mailed me the last jar of summer honey. Before writing this book, I had not really been a honey connoisseur, and I was not expecting it to taste different from the honey in my cupboard from the grocery store. I was deeply mistaken. After my first taste, I had to fight the urge to slurp it straight from the jar. I shared some with my friend Mary and some with my husband, but I'm saving the rest for a special occasion—perhaps some of Mary's homemade biscuits, hot and fresh from the oven.

Sarah Gayle

In 1831, John Gayle was elected the seventh governor of Alabama.[36] By all accounts, John had the perfect life—a successful political career, an adoring wife, two children, and another one on the way. But in 1831, success in politics usually meant spending a great deal of time away from home. So, Sarah Gayle, the governor's wife, had already learned to cope with loneliness long before her husband's election.[37]

While John traveled the state, Sarah remained at her home in Greensboro. When Sarah was living there in the 1830s, the town had a tailor, a few saloons, several shops, and a law office.[38] Even though Greensboro has never topped four thousand residents, it has come a long way from its rustic beginnings. The Gayle house is still there in a quiet residential area behind the quintessential white picket fence. It's not difficult to imagine Sarah in that house, tending to her children and waiting for her husband to come home.

Sarah Ann Haynsworth married John Gayle in 1819, the same year that Alabama became a state. Only fifteen years old on her wedding day, Sarah considered herself a wild girl who had to grow up fast once she became

Right: John Gayle, the seventh governor of Alabama. *Courtesy of the Alabama Department of Archives and History.*

Below: Rear and side view of Gayle House. Greensboro, Hale County, Alabama. *Courtesy of the Library of Congress.*

a married woman. Twelve years later, that child had become an anxious woman. Sarah was constantly overwhelmed, not by duty or hardship, but by love and fear. She felt a crushing weight of responsibility to stay alive and protect her children. If she died in the uncertain frontier life of Alabama, anything could happen to her small children. Both of her parents had died by 1831, and she had no brothers or sisters.[39] Therefore, if she died, the best she could hope for was that her children would be cared for by the women in her husband's family. And like most mothers, Sarah thought her children could not be cared for properly by anyone but herself—and certainly not by her sisters-in-law with their own wildlings.

Happily, she had many friendships to distract her from her fears of death. Every day retraced a version of the day before, with shopping, child-rearing, going to church, or just enjoying general social activities with her numerous friends.[40] Without them, she would have been alone. These friends certainly saved her from lonely days, and yet, even with her social activities, she still could be quite gloomy. She was depressed quite a bit, which led her to take a bit of opium, which caused her dental problems—again causing her more depression. The one thing that filled her with fear almost as much as death was losing her teeth and the affect it had on her appearance. She dreaded that her husband saw her as less than what she felt herself to be.

A few months after her husband's election, Sarah gave birth to a new baby boy in February 1832. Shortly afterward, her husband's sister arrived from Florida to set up housekeeping. Lucinda and her children lived with the Gayle family for a few weeks before finding their own home, although her husband remained in Key West, where he had an important job. Like Sarah, Lucinda was on her own a great deal of the time. John's brother Levin was unemployed most of the time, which worried his wife, Ann, to distraction, and the three anxious women spent a lot of time together.

Sweetmeats

On October 28, 1832, Sarah wrote this entry into her diary:

> *We all dined with Levin today, and a most capital dinner we had, which I did not enjoy as usual in consequence of having eaten very heartily at Lucinda's an hour before dinner, of her superb honey citron and grape sweetmeats, fresh butter with its accompaniment of butter and sweet milk,*

biscuit and coffee. What a thousand pities that one's feelings cannot remain calm, unsoured and in proper tone as they were this morning, and generally, at this little familiar social meeting! However, they will be remembered with delight long after any vexations, intervening circumstances are forgotten, as all such should be.[41]

What are sweetmeats? In early cookbooks, sweetmeats seem to be synonymous with jams and jellies, but in late nineteenth-century cookbooks, it becomes apparent that there is a difference. Any kind of fruit you see on the jam labels at your nearest supermarket can be made into sweetmeats, like peaches, strawberries, blackberries, or currants. Making them at home can be intimidating at first, but it's not as scary as it seems, provided you have some experience in the kitchen. For myself, I have my friend Mary, whom I have known since we were teenagers. Mary is an old-fashioned southern cook, which means that if something can be fried, she fries it—and really, everything can be fried.

Running her kitchen with a frying pan and lots of love, Mary is the perfect person to help with historical recipes. Even her children help us cook, and since even her seven-year-old has better cooking chops than I do, it works out well. We cooked sweetmeats from a recipe taken from *Good-Living: A Practical Cookery-Book for Town and Country*, written by Sara Van Buren Brugiere in 1890. Although the cookbook was published well after the era, this particular recipe is easy to follow:

> *BLACKBERRY SWEETMEATS: Allow 1 pound of granulated sugar to 1 pound of fruit. Choose by preference the Lawtons for this purpose. Put the fruit into a porcelain-lined kettle and set on a very moderate fire until enough juice is drawn out to prevent scorching. Boil until perfectly tender, 10 or 15 minutes at least; then add the sugar; mix very carefully, not to bruise the fruit. Do not boil again. Just as soon as the sugar is thoroughly dissolved, fill the jars as quickly as possible. Cover immediately.*[42]

We found out the hard way that if you add sugar too early, the results will be a delicious jam, not sweetmeats. On our second try, we nailed it. If kept in a dark pantry, these sweetmeats can be kept for several months. In our case, the blackberry recipe was chosen instead of grapes, as it was blackberry season.

After eating sweetmeats, jellies or jams just won't do. If taken by the spoonful, the gorgeous, thick syrup dissolves over the tongue, and what

Three jars of blackberry sweetmeats. *Author's collection.*

remains is soft fruit, rich and sumptuous. If eaten on a biscuit, like Sarah Gayle did in 1832, the syrup sinks in, leaving only the fruit on a pat of butter.

Even though Sarah described these treats as Lucinda's sweetmeats, in all likelihood, Lucinda did not make them. Wealthy White ladies oversaw this kind of labor from their enslaved workers, but they did not perform it themselves. Sarah's diaries are largely introspective, and out of her thousands of pages of writing, only a few meals were recorded, but she did not record any mention of her enslaved workers' meals, nor did she include her children's meals.

Sarah Gayle's relationship with her enslaved workers has long been a matter of debate for historians. The question at the core of this debate is how can one feel genuine affection for a human being who is also their possession?[43] The answer to this might lie in the definitions of *marriage*, *identity*, and *ownership*, which have all changed in the past 150 years. Sarah Gayle owned human beings, but then again, she was not a slave owner because the enslaved people she inherited from her parents were officially the property of her husband. In other words, when John Gayle left his wife for weeks and months at a time, she was in charge of the enslaved peoples who officially belonged to her husband, even though some of them had once belonged to her father.

In April 1834, Sarah lost one of these enslaved people, Rose, to tetanus. Rose had been her son's nanny. Two weeks after Rose had caught a splinter in her foot, she began to have spasms. By the time the doctor arrived, it was too late. It took Rose another three weeks to die. They put her in Lucinda's house, where Sarah stayed with her. Sarah grieved for Rose, and as Sarah said, "Why not?" Rose was raised with her own children, as it was typical for the children of enslaved persons and the children of their owners to grow up together, eat the same food, play the same games, even drink the same milk from the same breast. Most were not even aware that they were enslaved until they were old enough for their former White playmates to take charge of them.[44] Rose had been the "the playfellow of all my children," and yet she was old enough to be their nanny as well. After Rose died, Sarah found it endearing to see her children playing in the room where Rose's corpse sat, waiting for burial.[45]

A little more than a year after Rose died, Sarah died from the same disease. In July 1835, she went to the dentist to have teeth pulled and filled. She developed tetanus and died; it was her worst fear: she left her six children with no mother.[46] There is no doubt that her death was painful, as she had recorded the excruciating details of her friend Miss Dearing's death from tetanus about a month before Rose died. It took Miss Dearing two weeks to die, and she suffered dreadful spasms from the smallest event. "Poor, poor girl, what a horrid fate."[47]

There is a difference in the way Sarah recorded the details of the deaths of Rose and Miss Dearing. For Rose, she mostly wrote about how the death affected her. For Miss Dearing, she wrote about how the death affected Miss Dearing. Unfortunately, this was typical and presents a problem when learning the details of enslaved people's lives, including their meals. Sure, we know what kinds of ingredients they were provided with, but that's not what we are interested in. We want to know what they ate and how they felt about it. Most of the information included in this chapter comes straight from the people in question through their own diaries or letters. Enslaved persons were not allowed to write, so it is difficult to reproduce their thoughts, much less their meals from this era. As the point of this book is to reconnect with history through food—to actively participate in it—slavery presents a difficulty, because their lives were not their own. In this case, instead of active participation, perhaps a moment of respect should be given for those who went before us—those who did not have a say in their history.

How food was dispensed varied from plantation to plantation. There were no official rules to follow, and every slave owner implemented a system that they believed to be best. It was customary for enslaved persons to have their own garden plots, supplemented with fish or game caught in their spare time.[48] However, not all slave owners allowed enslaved persons to have their own gardens, as they thought this would lead to too much independence. This meant that they had to dispense all rations either weekly or daily. As for meal preparation, this was another area that varied wildly. Naturally, enslaved persons would have preferred to do all their own cooking, but this would have meant the owners had less control over the situation, so a general solution was to dispense all the food and assign one cook for the entire plantation.

There is a piece of slave history left to us from the abolitionists who wrote biographies about enslaved persons during this pioneering era. Their motives were to convince ordinary citizens that slavery was wrong, so these biographies are chock-full of propaganda. Today, propaganda would be unnecessary, as modern people generally agree that slavery is evil, but at the time, people still had to be convinced. Therefore, these biographies had to be seen as not completely accurate—they were flawed. They were not lies, necessarily, but they were skewed. However, it is most likely true that the accounts of the meals eaten by enslaved people are fairly accurate. Surely food needs no propaganda.

James Williams

The autobiography of James Williams in Alabama has been both credited and discredited by modern historians and publishers at the time. Ghostwritten by Quaker and abolitionist John Greenleaf Whittier, most of James's autobiography must be taken with a grain of salt. That being said, even if some of it was altered, certainly the food needs no extra punch.[49] James was born in Virginia in 1805. In 1833, his owner took him and 213 other enslaved persons to Greene County, Alabama. James never saw his wife and two children again, as they remained in Virginia.

Slave owners did this often. Children were separated from mothers; husbands were separated from wives. The sale of human beings was a normal event, and it could happen at any time, which altered the notion of family relations within the enslaved community. To keep the family unit strong, it was necessary to look beyond the nuclear family. Aunts, uncles, and

SLAVES!

LONG CREDIT SALE

OF

PLANTATION HANDS

FROM ALABAMA, WITHOUT RESERVE.

BY N. VIGNIE, AUCTIONEER,

Office:----No. 8 Banks' Arcade Passage, and corner of Conti street and Exchange Alley.

THURSDAY, MARCH 25, 1858,

AT 12 O'CLOCK, M.

Will be sold in the Rotunda of the ST. LOUIS HOTEL,

No. 1. ABSALOM, aged 28 years, Plantation hand, fully guaranteed.

No. 2. NED, aged 45 years, Plantation hand, fully guaranteed.

No. 3. TOM, aged about 46 years, Plantation hand, fully guaranteed, except having a defect in the right knee.

No. 4. BILL, aged about 23 years, Plantation hand, fully guaranteed, except a slight defect in one finger.

No. 5. FRANK, aged about 25 years, a plantation hand, fully guaranteed, except a burn on his back and right side.

No. 6. ALFRED, aged 35 years, plantation hand, a good subject, has worked in a Blacksmith shop ; powerful built man.

No. 7. POLLY, Negress, aged 23 years, No. 1 plantation hand and fair Cook, Washer and Ironer, fully guaranteed.

No. 8. GEORGE, Griff, aged about 23 years, good plantation hand and carriage driver, very likely and intelligent. MARTHA, his wife, aged about 30 years, Cook, Washer and Ironer, with her four children : NED, aged 7 years ; NANCY, aged 6 years ; HORACE, 4 years, and MARY, aged 1 1-2 years.

☞ All of the above Slaves are from the State of Alabama, and sold under a full guarantee, except the defects above stated.

ALSO, at the same time and place the following

LIST OF ACCLIMATED SLAVES.

No. 9. DAN, Black, aged about 23 years, a good Cooper, acclimated.

No. 10. LEWIS, aged about 35 years, general laborer, and accustomed to work in a brick yard.

No. 11. FIRMAN, aged about 40 years, general laborer, and accustomed to work in a brick yard.

No. 12. MARY, Griff, aged about 27 years, a good house servant and child's nurse, and No. 1 washer, and ironer, having absented herself once from her former owner.

No. 13. JIM, Black, aged about 26, a general laborer, and good subject.

☞ All the above Slaves are fully guaranteed against the vices and diseases prescribed by law, except the defects made known.

Terms---9 months for approved city acceptances, bearing 6 per ct. interest

A broadside for a New Orleans auction of eighteen enslaved persons from Alabama, 1858. *Collection of the Smithsonian National Museum of African American History and Culture.*

cousins became especially important in a community where any member of the family could be sold at any time for any reason. But at the same time, there was no real family, because family ties were not at the discretion of the people involved—they were controlled by their owners.[50] African influences still loomed large, and in African cultures, your place in your society is determined by your lineage. To not have kin was dishonorable.[51]

James Williams, dishonored and without his family, left home and began life over in Alabama as a roommate to Huckstep, the White overseer of the plantation. James also worked as his driver, which meant that his job was to push and whip the enslaved when Huckstep ordered him to. For the next four years, he whipped his fellow enslaved workers, hundreds of lashes at a time, and he watched Huckstep drink peach brandy at night.

One night, in July 1833, James and Huckstep had to set the dogs out to catch a runaway enslaved worker. Dogs were trained to tear apart runaway enslaved workers well before the overseer could catch up, so the sounds of the howling dogs would make any runaway jump in fear. When James and Huckstep did catch up, Huckstep ordered the enslaved person to be stripped naked and tied to a tree. After the runaway was completely drenched in his own blood from the horsewhip, Huckstep ordered James to prepare a salt-and-pepper bath to rub into the wounds. And then, Huckstep declared that James did not whip the women very hard when he was ordered to so; as a punishment, James was to be whipped 250 times when he returned with the salt-and-pepper bath.

James Williams had lost his family, his home, and his friends, and his sole purpose in life was to whip the other enslaved workers. He found himself with nothing left to lose—so, he ran.

Not long afterward, he heard the barking and howling of the dogs grow louder; except, this time, when the dogs caught up to him, they did not take him for a runaway slave, as he himself had been chasing enslaved persons with these dogs for four years. Instead of tearing him to pieces, the dogs licked him and received some timid pats before he managed to tear off their bells and send them running in another direction. After two days, James made his way to Creek Country, where he was taken in by Natives who showed him some kindness. They allowed him to rest until the following day, and they fed him venison, cornbread, and stewed pumpkin.

The ghostwriter makes little of this meal, but it takes very little imagination to think that, for James, it was probably the best, most delicious meal of his entire life.

4
ANTEBELLUM ERA

1830s–1861

PHILIP HENRY GOSSE

Philip Henry Gosse was one of Alabama's more unusual visitors. In 1838, he spent eight months in Pleasant Hill, a small unincorporated community in Dallas County. By pure coincidence, he met Judge Reuben Saffold on a boat sailing up the Alabama River. The judge was in need of a teacher for his new school, and Henry was in need of a teaching job. The two men struck a deal, and the man who would one day become one of England's preeminent naturalists spent the better part of a year in rural Alabama.[52]

Born in 1810, Henry grew up in Dorset on the southern coast of England, where he discovered at an early age the passion that would consume his life: the natural world. Growing up along the seashore, young Henry became interested in not only the marine life around him but the insects as well. Throughout his life, Henry was fascinated by insects, birds, fish, reptiles, and algae. He wrote over forty books and hundreds of articles on wildlife.[53] He discovered that when marine plant life is put into a glass container, it converts carbon dioxide into oxygen, which allows marine animals to be kept in the same container, far away from the ocean. Though he did not invent the aquarium, he did coin the word *aquarium*, and he wrote the instruction manual on how to build and keep one.[54] For the first time, it was possible for anyone to bring a piece of the ocean into their home.

PLEASANT HILL.

Pleasant Hill. *Courtesy of the Alabama Department of Archives and History.*

But all of this came later. In 1838, he was a twenty-eight-year-old, well-educated drifter in dire need of a profession. His father was a miniature portrait painter who could barely afford to feed his family. Although Henry had artistic talent, he had no intention of following in his father's footsteps. When he was still a teenager, he left England for the New World and worked as a clerk in Newfoundland for a company that traded with England. He then moved to Quebec to try his hand at farming but discovered it was impossible to make a profit. He worked as a teacher to make ends meet and came to the conclusion that it would make more sense to work as a teacher full time. Henry wrote, "My eye is towards Georgia or South Carolina, as I understand persons of education are in demand there, both in mercantile and academical situations."[55] It was not exactly a well-thought-out plan.

Philip Henry Gosse. *Courtesy of the Alabama Department of Archives and History.*

On his way south, Henry met an old friend who had an acquaintance in Claiborne, Alabama. With a letter of introduction to the man in Claiborne, Henry headed to Alabama, where he met Judge Saffold. This chance meeting with the judge was beneficial for posterity as well because Henry kept a detailed account during his eight months in Dallas County. His journal was written in the form of letters that were addressed to nobody in particular, although they were definitely meant for someone like himself—almost like an imaginary companion.[56] In these letters, he took care to describe not only the natural world but also the customs and culture of antebellum Alabama. He drew or painted 233 butterflies, dragonflies, moths, and other insects during his time in Alabama; all of these pieces have been preserved in the British Library. Auburn University digitized these drawings, and they can be found online at the Auburn University Digital Libraries.[57]

Henry could not get enough of the wilderness in Alabama. He saw "an inexpressible grandeur in these primeval forests."[58] His description of a loud, colorful forest is all we have left, since modern life has replaced most of his grand forests. On his walks, he saw wild black boar, wild turkeys, and red cardinals and heard the boisterous calls of the quails: "Bob White." Not content to just enjoy nature outside, he brought the wilderness home with him. After a sulky caterpillar committed suicide to escape being kept in a box, Henry was excited when a wasp made a home over the door of his schoolhouse. He forbade his students from killing the wasp, and every day, he made notations about the size of the nest and when the wasp brought friends home. On his daily walk to the school through the forest, he heard the sweet sound of a mockingbird in the trees; Henry was sure the same one sang to him every morning. He also enjoyed the turtle doves that not only sang soft, mournful songs but also made a tasty meal.[59]

Not limiting himself to the various birds and varmints that hunters shot and cooked, Henry saw the whole forest as his own personal smorgasbord. When there was enough sunlight on the forest floor, the wild sassafras trees grew delicious, bottle-green leaves that warmed his mouth when he chewed

Butterfly drawn by Gosse in Pleasant Hill, Alabama. © *British Library Board (add MS 89020/10).*

them. He snacked on wild strawberries, raspberries, and persimmons. He also ate figs from the trees in his garden, which were so luscious and sweet that Henry thought they were the best fruits he had ever tasted.[60]

Henry was simultaneously detached from his environment and sinking himself deeper into it. He had personal relationships with butterflies and wasps, yet he also joined in the hunts with his neighbors.[61] However, for

Henry, the hunts were more for his scientific curiosity than anything else. He recognized animals as living beings but also as things for him to kill in order to see how they worked. He had the ability to draw a beautiful butterfly and admire its beauty, and in the next breath, he would kill it in order to study it. This ability to detach himself from his environment while simultaneously being active in it is the reason he was able to stay in Alabama for as long as he did.

Henry had mixed feelings about the people of Alabama. Compared to the people he had met in the North, Alabamians were more hospitable and gracious.[62] Visitors were immediately given a glass of cold water, followed by slices of cool, pink watermelon. There was always plenty of watermelon to share with guests because every night, a cart from the fields was filled with watermelons for the following day. The fruits were stored away in an underground cellar so that when served, they were cool to the touch. No part of the melon was wasted, as the women of the house would cut the green rinds into stars and other pleasant shapes, candy them, and set them aside for a winter treat.[63] It's easy to imagine this custom of gorging on chilled watermelons during the blazing summer months, as Henry wrote that when the sun was barely up for two hours, the heat was already "scorching one's back and head like a fire."[64] Even today, the Alabama sun is still eager to begin the day with searing heat long before noon. But instead of watermelon and water, we give our guests sweet tea. For northerners and others unfamiliar with southern culture, sweet tea is always iced; there is never a need to ask for iced tea in a southern home.

Antebellum Alabama was also a very violent place. Henry saw duels, fought not only with pistols but also with Bowie knives, and in these cases, the victims were cut to pieces. In Henry's opinion, these duels were fought too easily and without good reason. He thought that slavery was the root cause of this violence, because if physical force toward one group of people was not only customary but expected, then by definition, violence was acceptable. Because of its easy acceptance, violence toward the enslaved population crept into other parts of society.[65] There came a time when he could no longer detach himself from his environment, and the screams from the whippings he heard from his bedroom became too much for him to bear. He left four months before his contract was up.[66]

In one of his early letters, written on June 1, 1838, he invited his imaginary friend to visit him for the day, and he laid out a typical day for this visitor to Alabama, starting with a meeting at the gate at 6:00 a.m. Henry wrote this day in the second person and invited "you" to spend it with him in Alabama.

In this way, he also provided reactions for his imaginary guest. In keeping with Henry's intention, you can assume the role of his imaginary friend and transport yourself to Pleasant Hill, Alabama, in 1838.[67] (In the interest of length and clarity, the following entry has been shortened and edited. There really is no need for so much information on waffles.)

"Walk in; we are just going to breakfast, though it is but six o'clock." You and Henry sit down to an early-morning meal of grilled chicken, fried pork, boiled rice, and hominy.

"Hold!" you say, "What is hominy?"

"Ah! I forgot you were a stranger. Hominy, then, be informed, is an indispensable dish at the table of a southern planter, morning, noon, and night. Indian corn is broken into pieces by pounding it in a mortar to a greater or less degree of fineness, as coarse or fine hominy is preferred, and this is boiled soft like rice and eaten with meat." As you and Henry eat your feast, he continues his discussion of cuisine in Alabama.

"Here is another article of southern cookery with which I presume you are unacquainted: waffles. You see they are square thin cakes, like pancakes, divided on both sides into square cells by intersecting ridges: but how shall I describe to you the mode in which they are cooked? At the end of a pair of handles, moving on a pivot like a pair of scissors, or still more like the net forceps of an entomologist, are fixed two square plates of iron like shallow dishes, with cross furrows, corresponding to the ridges in the cakes; this apparatus, called a waffle iron, is made hot in the fire; then, being opened, a flat piece of dough is laid on one, and they are closed and pressed together; the heat of the iron does the rest. They are very good, eaten with butter; sometimes, they are made of the meal of Indian corn (as so little wheat is grown here as to make wheat flour be considered almost a luxury), but these are not nearly so nice, at least to an English palate." Meanwhile an enslaved child continually waves a bunch of peacock feathers over the food, and over every part of the table, to keep off the flies, as these insects are so numerous here that they would otherwise settle on the food and spoil it.

"But I beg your pardon; while I am talking, you are eating nothing. Be bold; though strange, you'll find it all good. For drink, here is coffee, new milk (fresh from the cow), sour milk, and buttermilk—the last two are great favorites, but I dare say you, like myself, will decline them both: the sour milk is thick, and eaten with a spoon, so that perhaps I was wrong in calling it drink. Tea is almost unknown; coffee is the staple for morning

and evening meals. Here, too, is honey, fresh taken from the hive, and here are various kinds of preserves."

Even in his imagination, his friend is overcome with culture shock. "No more? I fear novelty has taken away your appetite; but, however, if you have really done, we will be going. I will just get my butterfly net and be with you; I always carry it."

Today, the Alabama breakfast is more likely to contain grits that hominy, but in December 2020, Mary and I attempted to make hominy, like that served at Henry's breakfast in 1838. It's easy to see why hominy was a staple. Dried corn was stored for the winter when food was scarce. Once it was cooked, this highly nutritious food could be eaten as it was, or it could be used in other recipes. Unfortunately, we chose to cook this dish during the height of the global Coronavirus pandemic, so we made it together over Facetime. Cooking with one of my oldest friends through technology made us each work together but separately, which is pretty much how everyone did everything in 2020. The most challenging part was actually getting the hominy, the dried corn. This was not sold in any local supermarket, and the traditional way of making it from scratch requires boiling corn in lye. We both vetoed that idea right off the bat, so I ordered some hominy online.

We looked at about five different recipes for hominy and decided on a combination of each recipe. Mary and I each took half a bag of dried corn, soaked it overnight, boiled it for three hours and then fried it with butter, salt, and pepper. We ladled the hominy into a bowl and took a taste. Sadly, hominy as prepared above, is painfully bland. That's when I looked back at Henry's account. "This is boiled soft like rice and eaten with meat." I concur, eat hominy with something—anything.

Nicey Pugh

When Franklin Roosevelt was elected president of the United States during the Great Depression, he promised Americans a New Deal. One of the programs fulfilled under his promise was the Work Progress Administration (WPA), but there were a number of agencies included in the deal. There was the Rural Electrification Administration (REA), National Youth Administration (NYA), and the Home Owners' Loan Corporation (HOLC).

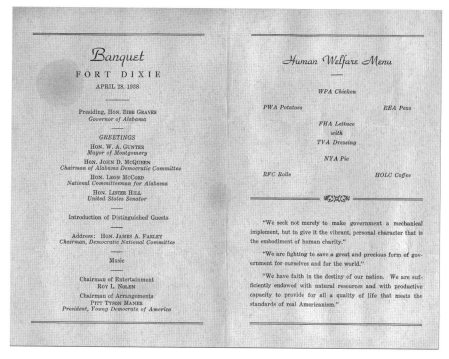

Banquet

FORT DIXIE

APRIL 28, 1938

Presiding, HON. BIBB GRAVES
Governor of Alabama

GREETINGS
HON. W. A. GUNTER
Mayor of Montgomery
HON. JOHN D. McQUEEN
Chairman of Alabama Democratic Committee
HON. LEON McCORD
National Committeeman for Alabama
HON. LISTER HILL
United States Senator

Introduction of Distinguished Guests

Address: HON. JAMES A. FARLEY
Chairman, Democratic National Committee

Music

Chairman of Entertainment
ROY L. NOLEN
Chairman of Arrangements
PITT TYSON MANER
President, Young Democrats of America

Human Welfare Menu

WPA Chicken

PWA Potatoes   REA Peas

FHA Lettuce
with
TVA Dressing

NYA Pie

RFC Rolls   HOLC Coffee

"We seek not merely to make government a mechanical implement, but to give it the vibrant, personal character that is the embodiment of human charity."

"We are fighting to save a great and precious form of government for ourselves and for the world."

"We have faith in the destiny of our nation. We are sufficiently endowed with natural resources and with productive capacity to provide for all a quality of life that meets the standards of real Americanism."

Human Welfare menu, 1938. *Courtesy of the Alabama Department of Archives and History.*

An Alabama dinner in 1938 had a little bit of fun with these acronyms and offered a menu complete with WPA chicken and HOLC coffee.

Among the many other benefits brought by the WPA program were the interviews of former enslaved workers, a project that became known as the "Slave Narratives." The Library of Congress has digitized these interviews and made them freely available on their website for anyone to use, which has been very helpful for historians and anyone else who wants to learn more about the lives and experiences of America's enslaved people.[68] However, there are certain flaws with these narratives—the largest being the use of dialect.

Most of the White writers tried to record the dialect used by the formerly enslaved people they interviewed. This means they used their own interpretations to record the voices of strangers. It may have been done with the best of intentions, but every writer used their own methods of documentation, and some of them recorded misspelled words for the sake of dramatic effect, not for the sake of dialect. For example, the words *no* and *know* have the same sound, but choosing to record *no* when the speaker meant *know* was not done for the sake of preserving a dialect.

Another challenge to consider is the time lapse; over sixty years passed before these interviewees provided the recollections of their experiences. Nevertheless, these memories recorded about slavery are still vibrant, even with these difficulties. One of the formerly enslaved persons interviewed was Nicey Pugh, and her memories were recorded by Ila Prine in Prichard, a predominantly Black city just north of Mobile.[69]

Nicey's parents were Hamp and Sarah West, and the family was enslaved by a man named Jim Bettis. Nicey was a small child when she was enslaved, but sixty years later, she could still recall the sounds of turkeys gobbling in the yard. She remembered a spring among the willows and the water trickling down the rocks. There was also a creek behind her house where cows strolled into the cool water for a drink. Dewberries were there for the picking, and she could reach under the shade of a peach tree and grab a ripe, fresh peach. At night, she fell asleep listening to the older enslaved people singing under the moonlight, and she woke up to the croons of the lark.

She also remembered what happened when the enslaved challenged authority. For the crime of sicking a dog on a cow, Nicey saw an enslaved man dragged through the town, hanging off the end of a horse, and made to walk over sharp stones with bare feet, which bled like he had been stabbed with knives. He was left to bake in the Alabama sun until they were ready to hang him. Before they did, they stripped him naked, threw stones at his body, and rubbed gravel in his eyes. Nicey told Ila, "I know it was a blessing to him to die."

As a little girl on the plantation, her labor included cleaning, sweeping, and building the fires to get breakfast started before the sun rose. All of the food was cooked in the open fireplace, including potatoes, collard greens, peas, and the meat of farm animals. Nicey's brother hunted at night, and the possums and fish he caught were also cooked in the fireplace. At Christmas, the enslaved barbecued a hog, and the women made molasses cakes. Mr. Bettis made beer, and everyone drank it throughout the holiday season.

Nicey was not sure what the beer was made from, but there were countless possibilities. Cull Taylor, a formerly enslaved man from Augusta County told his interviewer that they made good locust beer from locust seeds. They also made persimmon beer and wine from plums. On Cull's plantation, they grew rice, sugarcane, pumpkins, watermelons, cushaws (squash), peaches, pears, plums, and grapes. When they were sick, they drink tea made from sassafras leaves.[70]

Sassafras tea was a common remedy for illness, as was elderberry tea. Alabama's enslaved people had an intimate knowledge of the natural world,

Right: Nicey Pugh, age eighty-five. *Courtesy of the Library of Congress.*

Below: Young sassafras leaves grown in the Native Plant Garden at the University of South Alabama Archaeology Museum in Mobile, Alabama. *Courtesy of the University of South Alabama Archaeology Museum.*

and plants were used to make medicines as well as for food. Jerusalem oak plants were cooked into molasses candy and given to children to treat worms. Mullein leaves and pine needles were both made into teas for colds and fevers, but mullein leaves were also made into poultices and used for swelling. Roots of the mayapple were used as laxatives.[71] All of these plants are still around us, but most of us just see them as background noise, not ingredients.

Gaineswood
805 South Cedar Avenue
Demopolis, AL 36732

Serves treats during the first week of December as part of
Christmas on the River, a large celebration in Demopolis.
334-289-4846

There are some people who are blessed with inspiration and talent, and when those people are also blessed with good fortune, houses like Gaineswood in Demopolis are built. It took eighteen years for Nathan Bryan Whitfield and his labor force of both enslaved people and hired artisans to build this masterpiece. After Nathan's death in 1868, the house remained in the Whitfield family until 1923. Today, the residence is owned and operated by the Alabama Historical Commission. After nearly five years of careful restoration, tourists can visit the house and appreciate Nathan's architectural work of art.[72]

In 1842, Nathan bought a wood cabin and 480 acres from his friend George Gaines, and he named his house after his good friend. Years later, one of Nathan's grandsons explained that the house was built in the Greek Revival style, with all three Greek styles of architecture represented. The exterior of the house was built in the Doric style, the drawing room was

Left: Nathan Bryan Whitfield. *Courtesy of the Alabama Department of Archives and History.*

Below: Gaineswood in Demopolis, Alabama, which was built by General Nathan Bryan Whitfield. *Courtesy of the Alabama Department of Archives and History.*

made in the Corinthian style, and the rest of the interior was constructed in the Ionic style. Copies of antique statues, created in Italy, were imported for the house. In the drawing room, two mirrors stood opposite each other, and as Nathan's grandson says, it was important for them to be exactly parallel to each other so as to not distort the reflections. At the time, Nathan placed *Flora* by one mirror and *Ceres* at the other, both statues made from white marble. The statues, as well as every other item, were reflected thirteen times in both mirrors.[73]

This was the same year that Nathan and his wife, Elizabeth, lost three of their children to yellow fever. In 1846, tragedy struck the family once again: Elizabeth died of an intestinal disorder. In 1857, Nathan married his second wife and had his last child, Nathalie Ashe Whitfield.[74] Nathalie was sixteen years younger than the youngest child from his previous marriage, and it is because of her recollections that many of the details of life at Gaineswood are known, including balls thrown by her parents and the food eaten by the family. In 1977, Mary Augusta Whitfield put together a collection of Whitfield recipes, but first, she converted them into modern units. She included a few of Nathalie's recipes, including this one for crumpets:

54

Opposite: Gaineswood. Demopolis, Marengo County, Alabama. *Courtesy of the Library of Congress.*

Above: Gaineswood's interior. Demopolis, Marengo County, Alabama. *Courtesy of the Library of Congress.*

4 cups all-purpose flour
2 teaspoons cream of tartar
1 teaspoon salt
2 eggs
4 cups milk
2 teaspoons soda
melted butter

Sift together flour, cream of tartar and salt. Beat eggs until very light. Alternate adding flour mixture and milk to eggs, dissolving soda in last portion of milk and adding last. Bake on a well-greased, hot griddle or in a skillet in round cakes. Top while hot with melted butter.[75]

Titania Collette, Mary's daughter, made these for us. It was generally agreed by myself, Mary, both of her daughters, and even her neighbors that while they were not terrible, we would not make these again. They look like pancakes but are not sweet. These might be an acquired taste.

Gaineswood participates in a larger celebration called "Christmas on the River," which the City of Demopolis has hosted since 1973. The first week of December is dedicated to both Christmas and southern cuisine activities, including the lighting of the trees, a Christmas story read by Santa, candlelight tours of historic homes, and, of course, a barbecue competition. Thousands of people attend this event, which has become one of the top-twenty attractions in the Southeast. The highlight of the celebration is the nighttime Christmas parade on the Tombigbee River, where floats light up the sky before the fireworks finish it off. As one of the historic homes offering a candle-lit tour, Gaineswood also serves refreshments under the portico.[76]

5

THE CIVIL WAR

1861–1865

William Howard Russell

On the steps of the state capitol building in Montgomery on February 18, 1861, Jefferson Davis was inaugurated as the president of the Confederate States of America. At this point, there were only six states in the fledgling renegade nation: Alabama, South Carolina, Mississippi, Florida, Georgia, and Louisiana. Before long, this number swelled to eleven, and a larger industrial city was needed. When Virginia joined the Confederacy in May, the City of Richmond was offered as the capital, and Montgomery's time as the capital of the Confederacy came to a close after only four months. In early May 1861, days before the Confederate capital moved to Richmond on May 20, William Howard Russell, a war correspondent for the *London Times*, visited Montgomery.[77]

William was born in 1820 to a Catholic mother and Protestant father in Ireland, which probably meant he was no stranger to civil discord. He joined the *London Times* as a correspondent and started his career reporting on Irish matters, but before long, he was given larger assignments. In the 1850s, the *Times* sent him to report on the hostilities in Crimea.[78] His prime location when the war broke out, coupled with the new invention of the telegraph, gave him the best advantages to chronicle the Crimean War.[79] William's reports in 1854 brought England's inept military leadership into full view of the public. This led to reforms within the military, and his

William H. Russell, esquire, *London Times* special correspondent. *Courtesy of the Library of Congress.*

report on the Russian slaughter of British soldiers during the Battle of Balaclava inspired Alfred Lord Tennyson's famous poem "The Charge of the Light Brigade."[80]

> *Half a league, half a league, / Half a league onward, / All in the valley of Death / Rode the six hundred. / "Forward, the Light Brigade! / Charge for the guns!" he said. / Into the valley of Death / Rode the six hundred.*

These reports on the Crimean War made William famous as the first modern war correspondent, and when it looked like the New World was on the brink of catastrophe, the *Times* sent him to America.[81] William arrived in the Confederate capital on May 4, 1861, almost at midnight, after a day's worth of train travel from Macon, Georgia. When he checked into his hotel, he and three other travelers were given a room with only three beds, in which two other men were already sleeping. After some bribery and begging, the weary group managed to get extra mattresses from the hotel staff so that they would not have to sleep in beds with strangers. Although the room buzzed with flies and fleas, William was just grateful he was not one of the men on the mattresses because his neighbor in the next bed was a "tremendous projector in the tobacco juice line," and the poor soul on the mattress between them got besieged with the brown juice. The first modern war correspondent who had witnessed the carnage of the Crimean War spent his first night in Montgomery huddled under his mosquito netting with one eye open for fear of the man with the tobacco pouch.[82] First impressions are hard to shake off. As far as William Howard Russell was concerned, Montgomery never had a chance.

William would have agreed with Henry Gosse and his assessment of the violence in Alabama. He knew he was probably one of the very few people in Montgomery not armed with either a Bowie knife or a six-shooter. He thought the people of Montgomery were more coarse, rude, and physically larger than their northern contemporaries, and of course, they chewed too much tobacco. The streets were hot and unpleasant, but William still had reports to file. Onward he went, probably being careful of where he stepped. He went to visit the capital to observe the new Confederate Congress when he passed a crowd of people gathered around a speaker. He thought it was possibly a stump speech or a sermon, so he went to listen, only to find it was a slave auction. Slavery had been outlawed in England for several decades, so it was jarring for him to see an English speaker sell one human being to another.[83] (The following speech has been edited for length and clarity).

> *"Nine hundred and fifty dollars? Only nine hundred and fifty dollars offered for him," exclaimed the speaker, clearly exasperated.*
>
> *"Will no one make any advance on nine hundred and fifty dollars?" A man near William opened his mouth, spat, and said, "Twenty-five."*
>
> *"Only nine hundred and seventy-five dollars offered for him. Why, that's ridiculous—only nine hundred and seventy-five dollars…"*
>
> *Beside the auctioneer stood a stout young man of twenty-five years with a bundle in his hand. He was muscular, with broad shoulders, high cheekbones and a pleasant, though sad, expression. William struggled with the fact that for the sum of $975, he could be the owner of "that mass of blood, bones, sinew, flesh, and brains." The man was sold to one of the bystanders, and William watched him walk away with his new owner, still carrying his bundle.[84]*

Afterward, William continued his walk to observe the congress. When he stumbled onto splashes of brown juice covering the white stone steps

THE STARTING POINT OF THE GREAT WAR BETWEEN THE STATES.
INAUGURATION OF JEFFERSON DAVIS
As President of the Confederate States of America, in front of the State Capitol, at Montgomery, Alabama, February 18, 1861. The above picture is a fac-simile of a Photograph taken on the spot, while the audience were at prayer, and a few seconds after Mr. Davis had taken the Oath of Office, which was

and pillars on the front of the capitol building, it must have brought on a little PTSD from the previous night. Once inside, he walked up the steps to the chamber, only to be horrified to see the floors browned with more tobacco spittle. For those visitors who could overlook the offending brown blemishes, there were tables laid with "hams, oranges, bread, and fruits for the refreshment of members and visitors."[85] Whether Confederate or Union, it's difficult for us to imagine walking into our capitol today and grabbing an

THE CABINET OF THE CONFEDERATE STATES AT MONTGOMERY.—[FROM PHOTOGRAPH BY WHITEHURST, OF WASHINGTON, AND HISTON, OF MONTGOMERY, ALABAMA.—[SEE NEXT PAGE.]

Opposite: The starting point of the War Between the States. Montgomery, Alabama. *Courtesy of the Library of Congress.*

Above: The cabinet of the Confederate States of America at Montgomery in 1861. *Courtesy of the National Portrait Gallery, Smithsonian Institution.*

Left: Jefferson Davis. *Courtesy of the Library of Congress.*

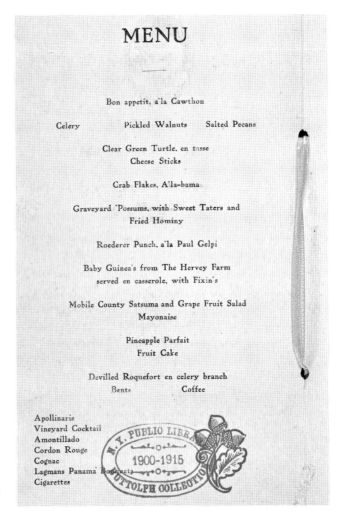

MENU

Bon appetit, a'la Cawthon

Celery   Pickled Walnuts   Salted Pecans

Clear Green Turtle, en tasse
Cheese Sticks

Crab Flakes, A'la-bama

Graveyard 'Possums, with Sweet Taters and
Fried Hominy

Roederer Punch, a'la Paul Gelpi

Baby Guinea's from The Hervey Farm
served en casserole, with Fixin's

Mobile County Satsuma and Grape Fruit Salad
Mayonaise

Pineapple Parfait
Fruit Cake

Devilled Roquefort en celery branch
Bents   Coffee

Apollinaris
Vineyard Cocktail
Amontillado
Cordon Rouge
Cognac
Lagmans Panama Bouquets
Cigarettes

Cawthon Hotel
Vineyard menu,
1913. *Courtesy of the
Rare Book Division,
New York Public Library,
Digital Collections.*

orange. In all fairness to William, it's also difficult to imagine walking into the halls of Congress and spitting tobacco juice on the floor.

The following morning, he read in the newspaper of the president of the Confederacy's proclamation of war between the Confederate States and the United States. He went to pay his respects to Jefferson Davis and saw the Confederate flag flying over the state department. The door was open. There was no extra bustle, just clerks going about their daily business. On the door of the second floor was a sign that read, "The President." Davis was in a meeting, but when that ended, he met with the Irish reporter from the *London Times*. They chatted about normal subjects, and William was pleased to note that the Confederate president did not spit tobacco. Davis was a gentleman, calm and resolute. He had a thin, wrinkled, intellectual face, with one eye that looked blind, though the other was dark and intelligent. He was neat, his hair was trimmed nicely, and his boots were polished. He wore a gray suit with a black silk handkerchief.[86] Of everything he saw in Montgomery, he wrote about Jefferson Davis with the most respect.

Not surprisingly, William did not enjoy every meal in Montgomery. The only one he thought fit to record was his first one, eaten at a restaurant near the hotel. "The bill of fare, which contained, I think, as many odd dishes as ever I saw, some unknown fishes, oyster-plants, 'possums, racoons, frogs, and other delicacies, and, eschewing toads and the like, really made a good meal off dirty plates on a vile tablecloth."[87]

Opossum is one of the foods that comes up again and again in Alabama diaries and letters. This must be addressed, but, dear reader, forgive me if this is the one recipe that I don't make myself. I do not relish the idea of cooking one of the little creatures who inhabit my backyard. I also do not encourage you to try this at home. The following recipe from *Mrs. Owens' New Cook Book and Complete Household Manual* (1899) is included for purely educational purposes:

> *Opossum: Clean like a pig—scrape, not skin it. Chop the liver fine, mix with breadcrumbs, chopped onion, and parsley, with pepper and salt; bind with a beaten egg, and stuff the body with it. Sew up, roast, baste with salt and water. In order to make it crisp, rub with a rag dipped in its own grease. Serve with gravy thickened with browned flour. Serve whole on a platter with a baked apple in its mouth.*[88]

Opossum remained a part of the Alabama palate for many years—if, indeed, it ever left. In 1913, a dinner was served at the Cawthon Hotel in Mobile that featured "graveyard possum" on the menu.

Parthenia Antoinette Vardaman Hague

In the summer of 1861, just a few weeks after William enjoyed his opossum in Montgomery, Parthenia Antoinette Vardaman went home to visit her family in Georgia. Her brothers had just enlisted in the Confederate army, and her father wanted all of his eleven children under his roof for what would turn out to be the final time.[89] Although no one understood the gravity of what was yet to come, it must have been a bittersweet reunion.

Parthenia returned to Alabama, where she worked as a schoolteacher near Eufaula in Barbour County. Eufaula was a busy town with two banks, several grocery stores, liquor stores, jewelry stores, tailors, and even an early version of a photography studio. However, once the war began, economic activity plummeted. The Union blockade eliminated the imports of clothing and food, which the South had come to rely on. Before long, there were shortages of everything, and storekeepers who had previously accepted credit adopted a cash-only policy. Starvation was a real possibility, as it was difficult to purchase food, even if one had cash, and most did not.[90] To make things even more critical, 10 percent of all food grown was earmarked for the Confederate army.[91]

Parthenia felt relatively safe from any war-related violence, as Eufaula was far enough away from both the border states and the sea.[92] Their isolation may have offered a degree of safety, but the Union blockade created other challenges for Parthenia and her household, as food and clothing could no longer be imported from the North. Years later, Parthenia wrote *A Blockaded Family*, in which she explained how her household had to learn how to make all the goods they had once taken for granted.

In the introduction to the modern edition of Parthenia's book, Historian Elizabeth Fox-Genovese says that although Parthenia and the family did have to learn how to survive without northern imports and how to make household goods at home, Parthenia did not endure the kinds of hardships faced by poorer Whites and enslaved persons.[93] People under different living conditions would have had a much tougher time than Parthenia, but her book chronicles how her family survived during the blockade. Her employer was the Garland family, wealthy slave owners, and the house she lived in was adorned with wide halls, a colonnade, and large, airy rooms.[94]

One of Parthenia's most difficult tribulations was the absence of real coffee. Coffee was an important drink, and some southerners drank three cups a day. Before it was gone completely, the price for a pound of coffee went up to seventy dollars, provided one could find any. In an effort to reproduce something like the coffee they had enjoyed before the war, Alabamians experimented with several substitutes. Some of these were imaginative and a bit desperate, and for those of us who had to fight for toilet paper in 2020, we can empathize with this. Sliced yams were cut into squares, dried, and parched. They also browned wheat and burned corn in an effort to get something that resembled the taste of coffee in their mugs.[95]

Barely four months into the war, Alabama newspapers were already advising ways to extend the dwindling coffee supply. The *Tuscaloosa Weekly*

Times ran an article in August 1861 that suggested to its readers that they could preserve their coffee if they substituted half of their coffee with roasted sweet potatoes.[96] The *Alabama Beacon* in Greensboro reminded its readers to dry their sweet potatoes in the sun for three days before using them to make coffee.[97] By the end of the first year of the war, the ratio of coffee to sweet potato grew more severe. The newspaper in Marion ran the following excerpt in December 1861:

> *I have tried the experiment of making coffee out of sweet potatoes. Cut the potato into small pieces—not too large to parch easily, and as near the same thickness as possible, so that all will parch alike—and brown and grind it just as you do coffee. Two-thirds potato and one-third coffee can hardly be distinguished from the genuine Java. It is certainly an economical drink, when coffee is so scarce and dear.*[98]

This desperation is in sharp contrast to a recipe for coffee that was recorded around 1850:

> *Wash the coffee clean and roast it to the color of golden brown and no more. Take the whites of 3 eggs to 1 pound of coffee and mix while warm carefully and transfer immediately to earthen vessels, tying them over with bladders airtight—take from vessels, grind it and place in a fine muslin bag. Suspend it in the pot, turn on the boiling water and cover the pot by this mode; it will be very strong, but it is best to drink by pouring on boiling hot milk.*[99]

For Parthenia, the best substitute for coffee was not sweet potatoes but okra seeds that had been browned.[100] As a drinker of triple-shot espressos, all of this sounds unbearable to me, but Mary and I made a valiant effort to see if this was possible. Our first batch of okra molded, but on the second round, we were successful. The okra seeds were dried, browned, crushed, and finally run through my French press using the same quantity I would require for regular coffee. The smell was not bad, and it did remind me of coffee. The taste was bitter and frankly just repulsive. But then I realized I had to add sugar and cream, and if I closed my eyes, it did, in fact, remind me of coffee. It's not something I would want to make twice, but Parthenia made coffee out of okra seeds from necessity because there was no real coffee to be found.

A bit more palatable are Parthenia's replacements for tea. She used blackberry leaves and huckleberry leaves for tea and their berries for jams and pies. However, her favorite substitute for tea was raspberry leaves. The larger problems were breads and cakes, but they soon learned to make syrup and sugar from the juice of watermelons and baking soda from the ashes of corncobs.[101]

Without access to northern medicines, the forest became southerners' pharmacy. For chills and fevers, they used extracts made from the bark of the cherry, dogwood, and poplar trees. For coughs, they made syrup from the leaves and roots from mullein plants and globe flowers. Laudanum was made from opium, which was developed from poppies grown for this specific purpose.[102] Laudanum was an important drug and was used as a painkiller; it was the same drug used by Sarah Gayle in chapter 2 of this book.

MOBILE
MOBILE COUNTY

Bragg-Mitchell Mansion
1906 Spring Hill Avenue
Mobile, Alabama 36607

There are two annual public tea parties: one in the spring
and one at Christmastime.
251-471-6364

In August 1864, at the Battle of Mobile Bay, Union admiral David Farragut shouted, "Damn the torpedoes! Full steam ahead!" And just like that, Farragut's words went down in history, and his victory cut off Mobile's access to its port and the outside world. It was not an easy battle. Farragut himself said that the Battle of Mobile Bay was "one of the hardest-earned victories of my life."[103] The Port of Mobile had been protected for most of the war, as it welcomed blockade runners with supplies for the Confederacy. The port might have fallen, but the city of Mobile stood firm until the final days of the war.[104]

Right before the end—and, of course, the soldiers involved had no way of knowing the end was near—Confederate major general Dabney Maury was in charge of the defense of Mobile, but the defense of the Port City came at a cost. In order to use cannons, Maury needed a wide berth, and the one hindrance to being able to see the enemy was the live oaks.[105] Even today, Mobilians take their live oaks very seriously. Should roots from a live oak damage the sidewalk, the sidewalk will simply be rebuilt in a way that won't disturb the tree. These trees can only be found on the southern coast of America, and northerners are usually shocked to learn how old southern oaks can be. It takes hundreds of years for a live oak to acquire limbs that can sweep across five lanes of traffic.

When a tree comes down, it's not just the trunk and the limbs, it's the shadows created by the breadth of the limb and even the light that breaches the empty spaces. When several oaks come down, the canvas of the city is changed. Mobilians did not appreciate Maury's efforts to "protect" the city. John Bragg would call it "Maury's folly" when the centuries-old live oak trees in front of his mansion were pulled down to make room for Confederate cannons.

Great naval victory in Mobile Bay, August 5, 1864. *Courtesy of the Library of Congress.*

Before he knew of the surrender at Appomattox, John Bragg took the acorns from the murdered trees and planted them in his front yard. A century and a half later, John's trees are still there, supplying the yard with much-needed shade from the Alabama sun.[106] Today, John's house is a historic house museum called the Bragg-Mitchell Mansion. Inside the house, most of the original furniture is from the Mitchell era of the 1930s, but there are a few pieces from the Bragg family. Most notable are the nine-hundred-pound pier mirrors in the ballroom and the marble fireplace mantels.[107]

Opposite: Admiral David Farragut. *Courtesy of the Library of Congress.*

Above: Upham family in the ballroom of the Bragg-Mitchell Mansion. *Courtesy of the Rogers-Rickarby Collection.*

There is some debate about when the Bragg-Mitchell Mansion was actually built. As nobody filed any paperwork or announced it in the newspaper, the date of construction is not entirely certain. It was certainly built by 1855, and it's possible it was built as early as 1847. Five families have owned the mansion; although, certainly more than five have lived there at one time or another. The final family, the Mitchells, wanted to preserve the house to be used by the city, and when it's not being used for weddings or special events, it's open to the public for history tours.[108]

Twice a year, in the spring and at Christmastime, a public tea is given. As a former docent at the Bragg-Mitchell Mansion, I have seen many afternoon teas. Typically, for an afternoon tea, southern women wear their Sunday best, which usually includes a matching hat, and men wear a coat and tie. Southern treats are served, and I confess, this is where I first learned about pimento cheese. I'm not talking about store-bought pimento cheese; I'm talking about thick and creamy pimento cheese, bursting with mayonnaise and just enough spice to make it dangerous, made by Alabama ladies who know what they are doing. There are homemade jams and chicken salad and, of course, enough crackers on which to spread as many

Afternoon tea at the Bragg-Mitchell Mansion. *Courtesy of the Bragg-Mitchell Mansion.*

Bragg-Mitchell Mansion. *Courtesy of the Bragg-Mitchell Mansion.*

treats as you like. Of course, there are cucumber sandwiches, but the real treat is actually the tea.

On the days of the events, the tea is simmered for hours until the party starts. The house smells of cinnamon, as well as cloves and citrus. Guests sit on Mrs. Mitchell's couches in the ballroom or at her bridge tables in the bridge room and sip tea from delicate teacups. With every clink of the teacups, you can imagine the sounds and smells of these rooms when Mrs. Mitchell threw tea parties of her own. I was not allowed access to the recipe for the tea until I had worked there for more than two years, and I'm not willing to share my secrets here. You will have to come have a taste for yourself.

AFTER THE WAR

1866–1900s

Booker T. Washington

The Civil War brought turmoil and starvation, but the period directly following it was filled with more chaos. The social and economic structures that had glued the South together were dissolved, and there was nothing to take their place. Wealthy White men and women who had relied on slave labor for their positions could no longer call themselves "lady" or "gentleman," according to antebellum standards.[109] Formerly enslaved people could come and go freely for the first time, and the questions of what to do and where to go had to be answered. Poor White people were no longer on the middle rung of the social structure, as they suddenly found themselves on equal footing with those they had always viewed as below themselves on the social ladder.

This chaos was not limited to Alabama; it affected the entire South. The federal government tried to reconstruct the South with its "Reconstruction" plan, although many southerners did not particularly welcome this input. There were no serious repercussions for Confederate soldiers, and even Jefferson Davis got off with what boiled down to be a slap on the wrist.[110] The former president of the rebel nation that raised arms against the United States went to prison for two years while the government decided what to do with him.[111] The newspapers sometimes reported his meals: "Breakfast—Ham and eggs, wheat and cornbread, butter, sugar, coffee, milk. Dinner—Mutton-chops, stewed oysters, potatoes, onions, apples, bread, butter, coffee."[112]

While the country went through a very hard time figuring out what exactly to do with Jefferson Davis, life was being figured out in Alabama. One of the biggest concerns for everyone was education. Black people had not been allowed to receive an education while they were enslaved, and now that they were legally allowed access to education, most of them wanted one.[113] Of course, wanting an education and finding the opportunity to get one were two entirely different matters. Before one could focus on education, one had to eat.

Born into slavery in 1856, Booker T. Washington belonged to James Burroughs, who owned a small farm in Virginia.[114] As a small boy, Booker's duties included toting water to field workers, cleaning up the yard, and fanning the flies off the dining room table.[115] He played games with the Burroughs children, but he also had to carry their books when they went to school. When Booker was not allowed to enter the schoolhouse, he understood that as an enslaved person, he was not allowed to receive an education. He recognized that White people considered it dangerous to educate him, which made him want to taste that forbidden fruit of knowledge even more.[116]

When freedom came in 1865, his mother chose to leave her former owners and join her husband in West Virginia. The family remained there for the next seven years, and Booker worked as an assistant to his stepfather in the salt mines, as a coal miner, and as a houseboy for a wealthy White woman, all the while, trying to get an education whenever he could squeeze a few extra minutes into the workday. One day in the coal mine, he overheard his coworkers discussing the Hampton Institute, a school created especially for Black people in Virginia. In 1872, with almost no money and no connections, Booker walked five hundred miles to Hampton to get his education.[117] What he learned there would change the landscape of Alabama forever.

Booker worked as a janitor to pay for his Hampton tuition. However, his nonacademic lessons at Hampton were perhaps even more important in shaping his teaching philosophy. The student body received lessons in basic personal care before they were taught anything else. He learned how to sleep between sheets and how to use a toothbrush, neither of which he had learned to do while he was enslaved or during his years in West Virginia.[118] Hampton Institute was meant to train teachers so that more Black people could have access to education. Hampton not only trained its student body how to be teachers but also how to work in industrial jobs. Students were taught the value of labor and how to take joy in one's work, as opposed to working through forced labor.[119]

In 1881 Booker was tapped to run a Black school in Tuskegee. Like Hampton, it was to be a normal school, which meant that students who

Booker T. Washington (1856–1915). *Courtesy of the National Portrait Gallery, Smithsonian Institution.*

graduated from Tuskegee would be qualified to teach students of their own. He was only twenty-five years old, but Booker had been teaching since he graduated from Hampton in 1875. When he arrived in Tuskegee, he found there was no school to run. He had to build the school from the ground up, which meant he had to find the students and construct the buildings, but first, he had to find the land to put both on. Booker was imaginative with all three; he borrowed money from a Hampton friend for the land, he found an old church to suffice for a temporary building, and, to find students, Booker roamed the Alabama countryside. He stayed in the houses of the people he tried to recruit and got a very up-close look into their everyday lives.[120]

Alabama's Black residents usually lived in small cabins, which reminded Booker of how he had lived as an enslaved person on the Burroughs Farm in Virginia. Fifteen years had passed since the end of the Civil War, but many formerly enslaved people had remained in the South to work in agriculture. No longer slaves, most were sharecroppers, which is what it sounds like. Instead of paying rent, sharecroppers gave their landlords a share of their crops. Cotton was still king, and in order to make a profit, sharecroppers had to grow as much as possible. Sometimes, cotton was planted right up to a sharecropper's front door, making it impossible for them to grow their own grains, vegetables, or any other crops.[121]

The families usually slept together in one room. Booker slept in the same room, although they usually made a special place for him on the floor or gave him a spot in someone's bed. Bathing and washing up was done outside in the yard. The sharecroppers' meals consisted of mostly pork fat and cornbread, but Booker visited more than one family who only ate cornbread and black-eyed peas. As they did not grow grains, they had to buy it to make the cornbread, and it was sold for a high price. A typical day began with the woman of the house frying both meat and bread for breakfast. Both her husband and children took their breakfasts to go, while she ate her breakfast in the house. The husband ate his on his way to the field, while the children had a quick bite as they played in the yard. After the breakfast hour, everyone who was strong enough to hold a hoe went to work.[122]

Black-eyed peas, sometimes called field peas, are a beloved southern food. They should be eaten with cornbread that has been doused with a good supply of butter. Soft, delicious peas flavored with garlic, salt, onions, pork fat, and other heavenly spices makes every southerner smile. I didn't need to get Mary to help me make these to know what they taste like, as I have eaten thousands of bowls of black-eyed peas. Southerners eat black-eyed peas and collard greens on New Year's Day to usher in good luck for the new year, but they also make a tasty side dish at dinnertime.

So many foods in this book are foreign to me, but when I read Booker's depressing words to describe a meal of cornbread and black-eyed peas "cooked in plain water," I felt like I was back in my mother's kitchen again. Black-eyed peas are a traditional southern dish, but to cook them without spices or flavors makes me feel a small connection to the sharecroppers in the 1880s because I know exactly what that meal tastes like, and I have eaten the same meal myself. Food cooked without spices or flavors is not enjoyable.

Roof construction by students at Tuskegee Institute, circa 1902. *Courtesy of the Library of Congress.*

Cutting sugar cane on the Marshall Farm. Tuskegee, Alabama, circa 1902. *Courtesy of the Library of Congress.*

In his travels through rural Alabama, Booker managed to find thirty students near Tuskegee. The student body grew quickly, and Booker needed real buildings. Whether for frugality, to instill pride in his students, or to show the world what Black people could do, Booker had the campus built completely through student labor. The only real difficulty he ran into was the lack of a brick supplier, so through trial and error, he and the students learned how to make bricks themselves.[123]

Booker wanted to empower his students, which meant giving them a skill that would earn them a wage. Some Black activists took issue with his approach to black empowerment, and not everyone approved of his methods or his philosophy. But his philosophy was based on his own experience in the world and on the time and place he came from.[124] Regardless of anyone's issues with Booker, he left a legacy of what can be done, as the Tuskegee Institute is now called Tuskegee University and educates thousands of Black students more than a century after Booker's death.

Lyla's Little House
4937 High Street
Mooresville, Alabama 35649

Sells desserts and candy.
(Usually) open on Thursdays and Fridays, 11:00 a.m. to 4:00 p.m.
256-476-4988

About three hours away from Tuskegee sits the miniature town of Mooresville. Today, there are only sixty citizens in Mooresville, which is four fewer than when it was founded in 1818. Many of the original buildings are still standing, and some of them are still used for their original purpose. The town has the oldest post office still in use in America, and some of the boxes have belonged to the same families for generations.[125] The entire town only takes up one square mile, and everybody knows everybody. "If we don't know your business, we will find out," one Mooresville citizen told me.

In 1890, almost ten years after Booker rounded up the sons and daughters of sharecroppers' children for his new school, Zack Simmons built a two-room cottage for himself and his wife Mandy. Zack was the town carpenter and obviously talented, because although the cottage is small, it is said to be one of the most beautiful buildings in Mooresville. Built in the Downing Gothic style, the porch has curved brackets and high vertical windows. Zack and Mandy were the descendants of freed slaves, and they made a comfortable life for themselves in Mooresville.[126] Every year, the couple threw a party for the whole town, and Mandy baked lard biscuits and made homemade jellies in the detached kitchen behind the cottage. The town's children who stopped by to visit Aunt Mandy knew they were sure to get fresh biscuits piled high with freshly made jelly.[127]

Today, the Simmons Cottage goes by the name "Lyla's Little House," and it is where Mrs. Lyla Peebles makes homemade ice creams, pralines, divinity, and other goodies. Lyla loves nuts in everything, especially pecans, and she puts them in everything she makes. She is currently trying to master macarons made with a pistachio ganache in the middle. She restored the cottage in 2011 and turned the tiny two-room building into a two-room shop full of delights for both adults and children. Lyla's Little House is only open on Thursdays and Fridays, except for when Lyla's grandchildren are visiting. On the Friday I spoke to Lyla, the shop was closed because she was frying chicken and making biscuits and gravy for her very fortunate grandchildren. It is recommended that tourists call before stopping by, as Lyla might be making divinity for customers, or she might be at home frying up chicken.

Mooresville is a small town that has their own way of doing things, but from what I can gather, it seems positively magical. Occasionally, the whole town gathers for outdoor dinners behind the church. Mayor Nikki Sprader is very laidback and chats easily and comfortably with writers while on her way to pick up her children from school. Every April, the town opens its doors with lectures and walking tours for tourists who want to see a town that has not changed much at all in over two hundred years.

Columbiana Inn
306 East College Street
Columbiana, Alabama 35051

Serves afternoon tea; reservations only.
205-669-1450

In 1900, John and Ada Pitts bought a three-room house from Clarence DuBose, the editor of the *Shelby Sentinel* (today, this newspaper is the *Shelby*

County Reporter). Over the next twenty-four years, the Pitts family renovated and expanded this small house into a Victorian masterpiece. John was a businessman and the county tax assessor, and Ada was a social butterfly. She was described as a lovely, quiet woman who grew roses in her side yard.[128] Ada joined women's groups, threw parties, and served as the girls' counselor at the Jacksonville State College for twenty-two years.[129]

To raise money for a new carpet for the Presbyterian church, Ada threw a "shadow party" at the house.[130] Shadow parties were all the rage at this time, but it took some effort on the part of the hostess. First, a sheet must be hung up across two rooms, preferably over a large arch. On one side of the sheet, the guests in the first room make shadow figures on the sheet with the help of a light set up behind them, and the guests in the second room guess what the figures are, as well as the person or persons making the gesture. These shadows were meant to be elaborate, as some magazines suggested enacting famous paintings such as *Washington Crossing the Delaware*, or *The Boston Tea Party*. And of course, refreshments should be served. In 1908, *Harper's Bazaar* suggested the following treats after the shadow games: "chicken patties, or cold chicken in aspic jelly, sandwiches (lettuce, caviar, pickle, and cheese), ices in flower forms, little cakes, fruit lemonade."[131]

In 1917, Elizabeth Talbot wrote in *Table Talk* magazine that refreshments for a shadow party must be black and white, as should any decorations in the room. Even the waitresses should wear black-and-white uniforms as they serve "very dark and very light cake, vanilla ice cream with chocolate sauce, sandwiches of dark bread and cheese."[132]

No one knows what kind of refreshments Ada served, but they certainly were as elaborate as these treats. Despite bad weather on the day of the party, there were enough Columbiana women at the party to raise thirty dollars for the new rug.

Today, you can still enjoy refreshments in Ada's house. Andrew and Diane Moore bought the house in 2002, and the restoration took five years. Today, they run the home as a bed-and-breakfast, but Diane also serves afternoon tea. Diane is a self-described "southern girl" who has come to love a proper afternoon tea. In the days before the pandemic, Diane liked to see her guests dress the part and kept vintage hats, gloves and even feather boas for tea drinkers to borrow. If it is safe to do so, Diane will return to this practice once the pandemic has passed us.

The tea is served in three parts. The first course is quiche, fresh fruit, and chicken salad, which Diane has named "panic chicken salad" because the first time she made it, she was in a panic, as she had never made chicken salad before. Her southern DNA must have come through in a

This page Columbiana Inn.
Photographs taken by the author.

pinch because it was a hit. She still makes her panic chicken salad, but she does it by heart, as she has no need to measure or write down her recipe.

For the second course, guests are treated to tea sandwiches, scones, and tea bread served with lemon curd and clotted cream on a silver three-tiered tray. There will be four sandwiches, but they will always be different. Only one of the four never changes—there will always be cucumber sandwiches. When I talked to Diane about her sandwiches, she clearly felt strongly about including the cucumber sandwich. She also told me that, for a long time, she had been unaware you could actually buy premade lemon curd and clotted cream. She seemed to think this was a bit sacrilegious, so I think it's safe to assume guests will always receive the freshest homemade breads, lemon curd, and clotted cream at the Columbiana Inn.

For the third course, each guest receives three desserts on an antique folding tray. Diane's signature dessert is a chocolate fudge brownie with cream cheese chocolate and almond icing. Diane serves the three courses in Ada's parlor, where you can see the same double mantle that Ada would have used in the early 1900s. Diane and Andrew have worked hard, restoring the house to its original Victorian charm, which is surpassed only by Diane's traditional Alabama manners. She speaks in charms and euphemisms, and her goodbyes will take twenty minutes at a minimum, so plan accordingly.

THE BIRMINGHAM YEARS

1900s–1940s

Bossie O'Brien Hundley

The city of Birmingham was founded in 1871, which makes it one of the youngest cities in Alabama. The city's natural coal deposits and easy access to the railroad made it a popular destination for settlers, and the city grew so fast, it was given the nickname the "Magic City." As the city sprang up, those who came thought it would "become a city of great expectations," as one new settler put it. The hopefuls came by the hundreds, even though, in the beginning, there was nowhere for them to go, and tents sprang up in the areas that are covered in concrete and steel today.[133] Houses, as well as a hotel, were built quickly to handle all the new arrivals.

By the time Birmingham rang in its first New Year's Eve, there were 800 souls there to celebrate the holiday in 125 houses. The people kept coming, and within two years the fledgling city's population had grown to 4,000 people.[134] That same year, the new city was hit hard with a cholera epidemic, which killed over 100 residents and frightened many others into leaving. The people of Birmingham who did stay did not cry over their losses. Instead, on December 31, 1873, they threw a ball to celebrate the end of the cholera epidemic. It was known as the Calico Ball and was attended by at least 500 residents who danced in calico clothing until 2:30 a.m.[135] The growth of Birmingham could not be stopped; it had only been paused temporarily. Between 1880 and 1890, the population rose over 700 percent to 20,000 people.[136] Today, with over 200,000 residents, Birmingham is the largest city in Alabama.[137]

Among the earliest families to settle Birmingham were the O'Briens. Frank and Indiana "Dannie" O'Brien moved their young family from Montgomery to Birmingham in search of new opportunities. When the epidemic hit in 1873, Frank refused to leave Birmingham and instead cared for those struck with the disease. Then he fell ill himself. His health became so poor that a casket was ordered for his funeral before he recovered. Because of his dedication to his city and its people, Frank remained a beloved figure until the end of his days.[138]

After moving his young family to Birmingham, Frank worked as a real estate developer, owned and operated a newspaper and built the first opera house in the middle of a cornfield. The townspeople thought he may have lost his mind, but Frank could only see the future and simply ignored those pesky stalks of corn. As always, Frank was right, and Alabamians traveled for miles to attend shows at his opera house. He was one of the very first to embrace the telephone and bought three lines when it was the newest technology to come to Birmingham. He also borrowed the first library book and installed some of the first gaslights in his opera house.[139]

On July 8, 1876, Frank and Dannie welcomed their fifth and final child into the world. Officially, she was named Julia McBride O'Brien, but no one ever called her that. As soon as the youngest O'Brien learned to talk, her nanny nicknamed her Bossie, and she was known by this name for the rest of her life. Bossie inherited her father's ability to adapt to change and see the future, and when women's suffrage became the issue of the day, she took up the cause enthusiastically.[140]

Bossie was elected president of the Birmingham Equal Suffrage Association in 1913, and the following year, she served as a chairperson of the statewide Alabama Equal Suffrage Association Legislative Committee. The Alabama suffragists had a bold goal: they wanted the Alabama legislature to put a suffrage amendment before the state electorate. In effect, they wanted the men of Alabama to vote on whether their wives and daughters should be given the right to vote. Bossie was the leader of this fight, and she and her group attacked it from multiple fronts. She sent letters and questionnaires to senators to find out their views and whether they would be in favor of proposing the amendment. If these men were not on the right side of the issue, she made sure they received educational materials to help them come to the correct point of view. She gave speeches, formed organizations, and ventured into rural areas of Alabama to engage

Judge Oscar P. Hundley and Bossie Hundley. *Courtesy of the Library of Congress.*

those who did not have other means of opportunity or access to participate in solving such issues.[141]

These excursions took her deep into areas far away from railroads, so there was little choice but to drive. Sometimes, a fellow suffragist would join her, but other times, she went alone. Bossie drove over unpaved roads without GPS when women had not been licensed to drive for very long.[142] With the help of local residents, she was able to pass out leaflets and set up meetings. In sharp contrast to the comfortable accommodations she found in cities like Mobile and Huntsville, she held suffrage meetings wherever she could, sometimes in cold halls lit by a single kerosene lamp. These trips allowed her to reach people she would never have reached if she had stayed in the cities, but they also gave her a deeper understanding of Alabama. She not only made connections with people she never would have met otherwise, but she also got many of them to sign her suffrage petition.[143]

Bossie's hosts were the same people who came to hear her speak. Though they did not have much in the way of worldly comforts, they shared with her all they had. On one trip through the "Tall Timbers," in the northern part of the state near Tennessee, Bossie stayed in a house where the supper included "coffee as bitter as gall, 'taters' cooked in the ashes, canned peas,

Bossie Hundley and her daughter Margaret. *Courtesy of the Alabama Department of Archives and History.*

and tall biscuits that were thoroughly raw inside. All of this revolved on a 'lazy Susan'—the first one I had ever seen." At another home, she was served "sow belly and a piece of lean." Bossie knew that her hosts fed her the best of whatever they had. She did not always sleep in bedrooms or even in beds; she slept wherever there was room for her in the small homes.[144]

In one home, when she tried to pay her hostess, the woman would not hear of it. She told Bossie, "Oh, I couldn't take anything. All of my life, I've somehow believed in the things you talked about last night and have never been able to help it along. If I can help by your staying with me last night, I'll feel that I've done something for the thing you're working for."[145]

Bossie's meals of uncooked biscuits in rural Alabama stood in sharp contrast to a tea she organized earlier that year. At a private club in Birmingham called the Southern Club, Bossie, in her role as general chairman, color coordinated an afternoon tea party in yellow, one of the colors of the women's suffrage movement. Bossie began the day in her own garden, plucking four dozen yellow irises to form into an enormous sheaf. The display of Bossie's own irises rested inside a wicker basket on Cluny lace, next to the display of yellow bonbons on the center table. Two additional tables had yellow mints, yellow suffragette wafers, and a bowl of fruit punch with chunks of orange sherbet surrounded by bunches of yellow roses. Yellow shades were used to soften the lighting at the tea tables, which were accompanied by assortments of yellow flowers. It must have looked as though a thousand yellow butterflies had landed in the room at once. Although the decorations were yellow, the suffragettes dressed in other colors. Bossie wore a white ratine outfit and a Panama hat. Bossie and her ladies also had suffrage supplies for sale, including stationary, postcards, ribbons, and gardenias. The tea was successful and well attended, with at least fifty people there to enjoy a dance after the tea.[146]

There are a number of cookbooks for suffragettes, but this recipe for vanilla wafers from *The Woman Suffrage Cookbook* (1886) might be fairly close to what Bossie served that day:

Vanilla Wafers

One cupful sugar, two-thirds of a cupful of butter, four tablespoonfuls of milk, one of vanilla, one egg, one and a half teaspoonfuls of cream of tartar, two-thirds of a teaspoonful of soda, flour enough to roll out very thin.[147]

Galley and Garden Restaurant
2220 Highland Avenue
Birmingham, Alabama 35205

Dinner is served Tuesday through Saturday, 5:00 p.m. to 9:00 p.m.
Brunch is served on Sunday from 10:30 a.m. to 2:00 p.m.
205-939-5551

In 1908, William Henry Merritt built a home for his wife and eight children on Highland Avenue, a quickly growing area of Birmingham at the turn of the century. Unfortunately, William died of pneumonia just a year later and did not live long enough to take pleasure in his beautiful new home. After his death, the control of his estate and his title as president of the American Bolt Company went to his widow, Mary Alice Merritt, who handled both positions, as well as her eight children, until her death in 1913. Like her husband five years earlier, she died in her own bed, and the funeral was held at home.

In November 1915, two years after her mother's death, Sallie Merritt married Marvin Wise at her home on Highland Avenue. It was a modest wedding at 8:00 a.m., with only friends and family present. The Merritt family had decorated the house with chrysanthemums, roses, and autumn leaves, and Sallie carried a bouquet of bride roses. After the honeymoon, she and her new husband were to live in the house her father built, though some of her brothers still lived at home with the Wise family for several years.[148]

Ten years later, in 1925, Marvin died in the house at the age of forty-five, leaving Sallie a widow with three small children. Other than the occasional deaths, the lives of the Merritt family were reasonably quiet. The family did not leave much to posterity other than their home on Highland Avenue,

Bird's-eye view of Birmingham, 1885. *Courtesy of the Library of Congress.*

The scene on Highland Avenue. Birmingham, Alabama. *Courtesy of the Alabama Department of Archives and History.*

The Merritt House in 1932. *Courtesy of the Galley and Garden Restaurant.*

several obituaries, and the occasional society notice. This makes the strange events of 1947 all the more fascinating.

In the summer of 1947, the son of William Henry Merritt (also named William Henry Merritt) was mysteriously murdered, and the scandal that ensued rocked Birmingham. The newspapers had a field day, as there was a missing murder weapon, searches for suspects, and lots of gory details. "Harry," as he was known to friends and family, worked for his family, helping operate Birmingham's theaters in the Merritt Theater Chain.[149] The newspapers reported that he surprised a burglar in his house at about 6:00 p.m. The killer shot at him once as he was standing in the doorway between two bedrooms. A few minutes later, he was shot three more times. Of the four shots fired, three hit him—two in the head and one in the chest. After being critically shot three times, he managed to stagger to his bed before collapsing on it. The killer then fled, taking the murder weapon and some stolen cash with them. A few minutes later, Harry's wife and neighbors came running, only to find his dead body in bed, covered in blood.[150]

Over the next four days, the newspapers recounted and rehashed the story, and every day, their adjectives became ever more inventive. By the end, Harry had been "a tall, husky theater man," who was "slain" in his "fashionable home" on a "swank estate."[151] Even the family dog made it into the paper: "If Barks Were Words, Cookie Could Answer," along with a photograph of the family dog who was hailed as the only eyewitness to the crime.[152]

Walter Simmons, an eighteen-year-old Black worker who was employed in their stables was arrested for the crime. The newspapers reported that Walter had come looking for money that Harry owed him for his work. In his confession, Walter said he picked up one of Harry's three pistols, which just happened to be lying on the table in front of him. He then opened the pocketbook to take the cash, and then Harry walked in from his own bedroom, the adjoining room. He shot Harry once and then later said he shot Harry three times.[153]

Walter was arrested and given a polygraph test, a contraption so new that this was the first circumstance in which it was used in a murder investigation in the city.[154] The test was declared inconclusive, as police said Walter had "a poker-faced demeanor." The suspect denied all charges for four days, but on the fourth day, he confessed. He led police to where he had hidden the gun and money, which was under a rock behind Harry's house.[155] During his trial that October, Walter told the jury that he had been beaten by men who had forced him to hide the money and pistol before the shooting even occurred. His lawyer told the courtroom that Walter had been beaten and starved by police, and that officers had promised him a light sentence if he confessed.[156] Walter was convicted of murder and sentenced to life in prison but was granted parole in 1969 in the state of Pennsylvania.[157] He lived the rest of his days in Pennsylvania, where he married and raised a family.

What really happened to Harry? I'm not sure, but in April 2021, Lesley and I went to brunch at the house where he grew up with his seven brothers and sisters. This area of Birmingham is still very attractive, even if it's a bit busier than it was a century ago. The house is both surreal and completely natural, as it looks equally like a one-hundred-year-old house and a restaurant on a modern street. This is partly due to the street itself, which looks both old and new. William built his house on a steep hill, but thankfully, Galley and Garden has a valet service, as I was not at all sure I had the ability to drive down the narrow, steep hill into the parking area behind the house.

Even though Governor Kay Ivey had revoked Alabama's mask mandate a few weeks earlier, everyone wore their masks until they were seated, and there were quite a few people there for brunch. It was a full house, but it did not feel crowded, due to the ingenious forethought of Galley and Garden. They have kept the original design of the house for all the dining areas; they've only rebuilt the kitchen and staff areas. This means that there are several small dining areas without any large dining rooms. As it is a two-story house with all the rooms utilized this way, they can fit quite a number of people in the restaurant, and everyone can still have an intimate dining experience.

During his rounds of the restaurant, the maître d', Stan, stopped by to see how we were doing. After a short conversation and an explanation of our agenda, Stan emailed me the gorgeous photograph of the house that you see in this book. He explained that although the fireplace mantels are new, the crown moulding is original, along with most of the windows. If you look carefully, you can tell which ones are original from the wavy glass, still there from when the Merritt family looked out onto Highland Avenue. Stan was not sure which rooms were used for what purpose, except for our small dining room.

Sallie Merritt Wise lived to be ninety-six years old, long enough to see her childhood home, as well as the home where she raised her own children, be turned into a restaurant. That restaurant turned into another one, and that restaurant became Galley and Garden. Years ago, Stan took her reservation, and her only request was to not be seated in the room where we were sitting because that had been her aunt's bedroom. Soon, the coffee arrived, and we sipped our coffees in Sallie's aunt's bedroom while we waited for the first course.

Lesley ordered a pickled strawberry salad, and I got a brioche with a bit of gorgeous, perfectly tart strawberry coulis. Both were delicious, and we ate every bite. The entrées arrived; Lesley had ordered chicken and waffles, and I had ordered oven-fired flatbread without the bacon or sausage, which left the eggs, cheese and herbs. It didn't sound very exciting, and I don't know what they did back in the kitchen, but this simple piece of flatbread easily fits into my top one hundred meals of all-time list. (Yes, I actually keep a running list in my head. It includes coffee in Italy, appetizers made by my sister-in-law in Bangladesh, and a sandwich I had in an airport in Dubai). Dessert arrived, and this is when Lesley lost her ability to speak. Her cheesecake literally rendered her speechless, which I had never seen before in our decade-long friendship. I ordered the chocolate mousse, as our waiter had told us it was the least popular dessert. I can understand why Lesley lost her words because the mousse was perfect—light and rich at the same time, creamy and chocolatey, delicious.

When we left, we were the perfect amount of full. We had eaten everything on our plates, and we were satisfied and happy. As Lesley and I waited for the valet to come back with the car, we noticed the exterior of the restaurant looks almost the same as the picture Stan had given me—except for the enclosures they have added to the front of the house. The enclosed area in the front is there to protect the garden, which Stan was tending when we left. This maître d' loves what he does, and it shows. During the initial COVID outbreak, when the state was shut down, Stan spent his time painting watercolors. Before everything opened back up, he took down whatever paintings the restaurant had displayed before and hung his own. They are quite good, and knowing who painted them and why makes them more special. I will definitely be going back the next time I pass through Birmingham. Frankly, I just want to taste that cheesecake.

BIRMINGHAM
JEFFERSON COUNTY

Redmont Hotel (The Harvest/The Roof)
2101 Fifth Avenue North
Birmingham, Alabama 35203

Meals or drinks
Call or check website for hours
205-957-6828

When the Redmont Hotel opened in 1925, it advertised modern amenities, such as circulating iced water, electronics, and bathtubs in every room. Birmingham's newest attraction was fourteen stories high with 235 rooms, each equipped with the best possible rugs and furnishings. In addition to the barbershop and the cigar stand, there was a twenty-four-hour coffee shop that catered to both guests and locals.[158] For several years, the coffee shop was advertised to Birmingham residents as the perfect place to bring a date after an evening of dancing or the family for Sunday dinner. The Redmont also offered a space for locals to hold luncheons, private dinners, and bridge parties.[159] In 1935, they advertised an elaborate Thanksgiving dinner for seventy-five cents per person:

> *Fresh Shrimp, oyster, crab meat or fruit cocktail, celery hearts, olives, consommé, pedapore, pilgrim mulligatawny, filet of sole, tartar sauce, saratoga chips, roast alabama turkey, chestnut dressing, cranberry jelly, roast loin of pork, apple sauce, prime ribs of beef, au jus, escalloped oysters, spiced yams, steamed broccoli, wild rice, brussels sprouts, fresh spinach with egg, hot rolls, bran muffins, tea biscuits, head lettuce, roquefort or thousand island dressing, asparagus tips, au vinaigrette, fruit salad, hot or cold mince pie, pumpkin pie, charlotte russe, english plum pudding, brandy sauce, chocolate, vanilla or lemon ice cream, boiled custard, coconut layer cake, ambrosia, after dinner mints, coffee, tea, milk.[160]*

When deciding what to cook for this chapter, Mary asked if we could make something fun, as she did not want to make any more hominy or crumpets—a fair request. We talked about the possibilities from this Thanksgiving menu, and Mary said she had eaten plenty of ambrosia at church picnics during her childhood. I vaguely remembered this dish being made with fruit salad with marshmallows. This was not really what I had in mind for this book, but Mary helped me make coffee out of okra seeds, so I really had no room to argue.

However, after looking up old recipes, it seems that marshmallows in ambrosia is a new invention. There were several variations of ambrosia, but the older ones were much simpler than the newer ones. Finally, it was something I could cook by myself. (OK, the more correct description is that I could prepare it by myself.) I layered sliced oranges and shredded coconut. The older recipes call for sugar as well, but shredded coconut can be bought already sweetened. After a little hesitation, my husband ate every bite. The tangy oranges and tropical coconut flavors make for a really nice combination. I can see why the recipe got convoluted as time went on. You can't sell too many cookbooks with a three-ingredient recipe.

Hotel Redmont, Birmingham, Ala.

Redmont Hotel. *Courtesy of the Alabama Department of Archives and History.*

In 1937, the coffee shop was replaced by the Rainbow Room, a name chosen because of the hundreds of lightbulbs hidden in the ceiling that made the walls shimmer with color. This added to the effects given off by the more than three hundred colored bulbs that were used for indirect light. The furnishings were black and gold, while the carpeting was red, blue, and gold.[161] These motley color schematics were meant to be elegant, although the design might seem garish to modern tastes.

The Redmont was on the cutting edge of the newest culinary trends in America, and on January 11, 1940, visitors to the Rainbow Room could eat all they wanted from the new smorgasbord for seventy-five cents. The smorgasbord had just been introduced to American palates the year before, when it was used as a platform to show off Swedish foods at the World's Fair in New York. In 1940, this would have been the first time that diners at the Rainbow Room would have experienced what has since become our modern American buffet.[162]

Today, the Redmont Hotel is still serving delicious food at the Harvest Restaurant in the lobby, but at night, patrons can visit the Roof, a rooftop bar where you can relax with a local beer and enjoy the Birmingham skyline. At the time of this writing, the hours of both the Harvest and the Roof have been minimized due to COVID, but they are expecting to open to full capacity by the end of 2021, assuming the pandemic is under control. Today, lunch or drinks at the Redmont Hotel look similar to the lunches and drinks enjoyed there in the 1920s, as the original chandelier is still hanging in the lobby, along with the original marbling. The original marble staircase has also been preserved, and when guests take the elevator to the Roof, they should make time to admire the original Art Deco from the 1920s.[163] Put on your flapper gear and go.

8

WORLD WAR II AND BEYOND

1940s

POINT CLEAR
BALDWIN COUNTY

The Grand Hotel
One Grand Boulevard
Point Clear, Alabama 36564

Breakfast is served in the Grand Hall.
There are multiple dining options here. Not all are historical. All are delicious.
251-928-9201

In Baldwin County, about half an hour's drive from the city of Mobile, there is a tiny stretch of towns called Fairhope and Daphne. Fairhope, in particular, is a tourist's dream; there are no chain stores, only mom-and-pops line the small streets. There are high-end antique stores, as well as affordable ones, garden stores, chocolate shops, and ice cream shops, and access to all of this is possible in just a few hours of strolling. Once you've eaten your ice cream and bought a few antiques, you can finish the day on the pier and enjoy a tasty seafood dinner.

However, for the more adventurous traveler, there is an even smaller, unincorporated community just a few minutes past downtown Fairhope called Point Clear. On a map of Mobile Bay, in the tiny spot where the earth was fashioned into a docked sailboat, a few hundred years of history and tradition have come to pass on the shore. In 1847, Mr. F.H. Chamberlain built a hotel with forty rooms and two wharves, one for men and one for women, as it was unheard of for men and women to swim together. There was also a separate dining room, as well as a detached bar called the "Texas," a common moniker for buildings removed from the others, like the state of Texas at the time. This original hotel is no longer standing, as there have been fires, hurricanes, and several different owners, including a few who razed the previous hotel in order to build something more elaborate.[164] But the one consistency in Point Clear is that there has always been a hotel that has had the best of everything the era could offer.

The hotel on Mobile Bay has been an integral part of American history. During the Civil War, it was used as a Confederate hospital, and the three hundred soldiers who died there were buried in Confederate Rest Cemetery, only a mile away. During World War II, it took on an even more important role as a training center for the United States Army Air Force.

Point Clear Hotel. Point Clear, Alabama, circa 1910. *Courtesy of the Alabama Department of Archives and History.*

Grand Hotel and beach. Point Clear, Alabama, circa 1940. *Courtesy of the Alabama Department of Archives and History.*

In 1944, Colonel Matthew Thompson paid the hotel one dollar to use the building as a headquarters for the top-secret military operation known as Operation Ivory Soap. That particular code name was chosen because Ivory Soap floats, just like the soldiers who were trained in the waters at the Grand Hotel.

Over the course of the operation, over five thousand soldiers were trained in Point Clear. The men arrived five hundred at a time, and during their two-week training sessions, they learned basic seamanship and maintenance, and to pass the class at the end of every course, each man had to "abandon ship" by jumping off a twenty-four-foot-tall tower into Mobile Bay. For a small community like Point Clear, the "top-secret" aspect of the mission did not last long, and the soldiers were incorporated into the lifeblood of the population. Soldiers joined locals for picnics and dinners, and they attended lectures and dances.[165]

Dining at the Grand Hotel in the 1940s and 1950s was full of culinary delights for patrons. The menu changed every day, although there were certain special features that were incorporated into every meal. For example, an attendant offered an assortment of relishes from a tray at each table, and diners served themselves. Another attendant carried a bread warmer and guests chose from an assortment of fresh breads. One patron who still

Operation Ivory Soap at the Grand Hotel. Courtesy of the Grand Hotel.

remembers these days fondly from her childhood says that her favorite bread to choose was the corn stick, cornbread baked into the shape of a log instead of a muffin. Tradition also came in the form of music, and the Jack Normand Band played in the dining room for more than forty years. After Jack's death, his sons carried on his legacy and played for guests of the Grand Hotel until 2001.

Distinctive drinks were offered as well. On January 12, 1942, the Grand Hotel highlighted this on its menu. This drink is similar to eggnog and is typically enjoyed during the Christmas season.

> *Tom and Jerry: Beat four eggs until very light. In each glass, put three tablespoonfuls of the beaten egg, two teaspoonfuls of sugar and three tablespoonfuls of whisky, add a pinch of ground cloves, allspice and cinnamon and mix well. Fill the glasses up with boiling water and serve as soon as it is cool enough to drink.*[166]

Today, the Grand Hotel lies on more than five hundred acres and boasts more than four hundred rooms, ten times more than the original hotel offered in 1847. There are two restaurants inside the hotel, the Bayside Grill and Southern Roots. However, breakfast and Sunday brunch can be eaten in the Grand Hall, which was originally the dining room in 1940s. The chefs try to use local foods as much as possible to provide an authentic local experience. Blueberries are brought in from Weeks Bay Plantation in Fairhope; oysters come from oyster farmers in South Mobile Bay; crab meat comes from Barbour Seafood in Bayou La Batre; seafood comes from Bon Secour Fisheries; beer comes from Fairhope Brewing Company; and Dettling Bourbon comes from Atmore. There are beehives across the street that provide fresh honey when needed. Once a week, Claude's grits are bought from Ken Jansen, who has been grinding corn for the Grand Hotel and other Point Clear locals for years, just like his father Claude before him. Other vegetables and herbs are grown in the garden behind Southern Roots. And, of course, like all good Alabama natives, the chefs only serve Conecuh sausage. For readers outside of Alabama, Conecuh sausage is revered almost as much as football is in this state, so, if possible, this is one Alabama specialty you should not miss.

In April 2021, my friends Carol and Amy met me for breakfast at the Grand Hotel, the same area that served as the dining room for the soldiers in 1944. Carol is a fellow historian who has actually edited large parts of this book, and Amy is the chief financial officer for the City of Pensacola. Unfortunately, I was late to my own breakfast because the complex is a lot larger than I had imagined. After several wrong turns and a few panic attacks, I found my way to the historic building, which was actually clearly labeled.

Eventually, I made it to breakfast, where Carol and Amy were already sipping coffee. It was much busier than I thought it would be, and the hall buzzed with the large number of guests and servers running here and there. Carol and Amy both ordered the buffet, with promises to sacrifice their waistlines so that they could taste and report on everything. I secretly counted. They both got four plates of food before we left and had no trouble making their sacrifice. Since I had only ever tasted grits from a box, I was eager to taste stone-ground grits. The difference was obvious from the moment the bowl arrived on the table; the grains were much larger and fluffier than anything I had seen before on any Alabama table. Perhaps if I had eaten grits like these in my childhood, I would have eaten more southern foods. The effort that the chefs go through to procure these grits is worth it, and I finished my first ever bowl of grits. Also on the table were my fried potatoes and waffle, and the girls brought back fresh cinnamon rolls, bacon, sausage and gravy, biscuits and eggs, and there was even a smoothie that Carol thought was "good but tastes too healthy." The only thing that was in debate was the sausage gravy. Originally from Huntsville in northern Alabama, where Conecuh sausage is not as prevalent as it is down here, Carol disagreed with their use of it in the sausage gravy. A spirited discussion about the uses for different kinds of sausage took up the next twenty minutes or so, with us agreeing to disagree. I guess everyone can have their own opinions, however blasphemous they might be.

Breakfast in the Grand Hall looks out onto Mobile Bay, so while we ate our delicious Conecuh sausage, we watched the slow-moving waves shuffle to the horizon. After breakfast, we walked outside, which was the dessert after the meal. The shoreline looked exactly how it does in the photographs online, but somehow, it's even more beautiful. We walked along the pier, along with dozens of hotel guests who were also enjoying a nice walk after a good meal.

Clyde May

Clyde May came home from World War II in 1945 with a purple heart. He had been shot in both feet with machine gun fire while marching down a hill on Guam. He never talked about the war with his family because he said that war was about fighting and killing, and he did a lot of both. Clyde and his wife, Cynthia, raised eight children on Rabbit Road in the Almeria Community in Bullock County. The unpaved country road got its name because it was said that the only creatures who bothered to go there were rabbits.[167]

Clyde bought several acres of land and tried to grow various crops, but eventually, he declared his land only suitable for raising "pine trees, sandspurs, peanuts, younguns, and fine moonshine whiskey." Of course, the profit margin was largest for the whiskey. Clyde had a strong ethical and moral code, but it was not always up to par with the laws of the state of Alabama. The tradition of making moonshine goes back several generations and is passed from father to son, just as Clyde taught his own sons to make moonshine before they were old enough to drive. One of his sons, Kenny May, was the one responsible for sharing his father's story, and Alabama historian Wade Hall recorded it in his book *Waters of Life from Conecuh Ridge: The Clyde May Story*.[168]

Clyde was born and raised during the Great Depression, and he understood hunger and poverty. His mother died when he was six years old, and his grandparents raised him as one of their own, so his aunts and uncles became like his brothers and sisters. His grandparents did not always have enough food, and Clyde felt like an intruder when he ate food that might have gone to his grandparents' small children. Clyde was determined that his own eight children would feel wanted, loved, and definitely fed.[169]

Clyde's table welcomed anyone who came for dinner. Cynthia cooked from memory and instinct—never from a cookbook. She baked mouthwatering buttermilk biscuits, red velvet cakes, German chocolate cakes, and fruitcakes from scratch. Of course, she fried anything that could be fried. The table was laid with more food than the family could eat, just in case they had unexpected visitors, which they often did. Dinner may have only been cornbread and peas, but there were always extra portions on the table. The family grew most of their own food, just like everyone else in their community. Cynthia and the girls canned the vegetables from the garden so that the family and guests could have corn, peas, tomatoes, and butterbeans during the winter months. The boys milked cows, which provided the family fresh milk and butter. Sometimes, in the winter, Clyde would barbecue a pig over a pit in the backyard—often for up to eighteen hours—and the entire community was invited to come share the feast.[170]

The church played a large role in country life, and the May family attended Macedonia Baptist Church. They attended preaching year-round, but the biggest day for the church was the Fourth of July celebration. From the days following the end of the Civil War, the church held a Fourth of July singing celebration called Sacred Harp.[171]

Sacred Harp is a primitive singing tradition that is hundreds of years old. It was started in England, traveled to colonial America, and eventually found its home in the American South, where it is still practiced today. There are no instruments—not even a harp—but a large group of people singing in four-part harmony. Singers are separated into four sections—soprano, alto, tenor, and bass—formed in the shape of a square, with the leader in the center of the "hollow square." People who sing Sacred Harp music do not perform for an audience; they perform for themselves and each other. The music would not be described as sweet but stirring, raw, and powerful.[172]

This was an important day in the May family, second only to Christmas. In addition to singing and preaching, the food was a huge part of the day. Clyde barbecued pork the day before the event in a barbecue pit at the Almeria Schoolhouse. Others in the community brought food as well, and there was barbecued pork, fried chicken, vegetables, cakes, and pies. The food was spread on long tables, and everyone ate together. Throughout the day, the men would escape into the woods to drink moonshine, and certainly, some of that moonshine was made by Clyde and his sons.[173]

Clyde was not the only moonshiner in Bullock County, but he was known to make the best. Clyde's strong ethics extended to his moonshine, too, and he never sold a bad batch. Clyde said, "There's only good whiskey and bad whiskey. I make only good whiskey. If I ever made a bad run of whiskey, no one ever knew it. I poured it out. No one ever had a chance to drink it." He

A.M. Cagle of Villa Rica, Georgia, leading a song he composed at the annual Sacred Harp Singing at the Cullman County Courthouse in Cullman, Alabama. *Courtesy of the Alabama Department of Archives and History. Donated by Alabama Media Group. Photograph by Whaley, Birmingham News.*

made moonshine for over forty years and was only arrested once. For the crime of operating an illegal still, he served eight months of an eighteen-month prison sentence in 1973. On the day he got out, he set up his still again.[174] It is still illegal to make moonshine in the state of Alabama, so I will not be demonstrating this or encouraging others to do so. In fact, I say unequivocally: do not try this at home.

That being said, Clyde had a thorough system set up for his moonshine. Just as the land provided soil for his vegetables, tree limbs from the piney woods in Bullock County provided shelter for his stills. Clyde kept his operation deep in these woods, far away from prying eyes. He also used water from the springs along the Chunnenuggee Ridge, which was naturally filtered by the white sandy soil. Clyde would always put his stills close to running water because stagnant water would not make good whiskey. The water had to be pure and fresh, and for that, it needed to flow. He used rye from the Dakotas because of its larger grain, and he used yeast and lots of sugar. Unlike other moonshiners, he never chopped up his grains to speed up fermentation; he used the whole grains and let them ferment naturally. The rye grains were then covered with water and yeast and left to enlarge in barrels for a few days. Then heated water was poured over the rye, and finally, the sugar was added. Then the warm barrels were left to ferment in the sun. The mixture was then put into the still where it cooked. The alcohol turned to steam, which was then converted to liquid and put into gallon jugs.[175]

Clyde also made a special batch of whiskey called his "Christmas whiskey," which took a lot longer to make. He poured his moonshine into charred oak barrels, which gave it a caramel color. He also added charred oak chips and some slow-baked Washington apples, which mellowed the taste. These oak barrels would be put away in the fall and aged for a year, which is a lot longer when the hot sun of Alabama is taken into account. It was ready by the next Christmas.[176]

Clyde died in 1990, but his name and Christmas whiskey are still with us. Kenny May tried keep his father's legacy alive, and using Clyde's methods and Christmas whiskey recipe, he made the venture larger and legal. In other words, he paid taxes and adhered to industry protocol.[177] For a time, he was successful, but in the end, he lost his business. Today, Clyde May's Alabama Style Whiskey is operated out of a company based in New York City.[178] Today, Clyde's face can be seen on whiskey bottles all over the country. His illegal operation that was a natural part of him—no different from the pig he butchered or the crops he raised—has been made into a legal product. As part of my research, I bought a bottle of Clyde May's Alabama Style Whiskey, and I have to tell you, it's worth the hype.

Kenny was mistaken about his father's legacy. It was never the whiskey that made his father special; it was the life he led. It was the children he raised, the people he touched and the community he loved and cared for. And Kenny's legacy is the preservation of these things. Without Kenny's diligent efforts, Clyde would have been forgotten like the scores of other Alabama moonshiners who were trying to make better lives for their own families.

CIVIL RIGHTS

1950s–1960s

GEORGIA GILMORE

At 7:00 a.m. on December 21, 1956, Dr. Martin Luther King Jr. and Reverend Ralph Abernathy started the day by making front-page news on newspapers across America. They rode the bus.

"Is this the reverend?" The bus driver asked.

"That's right," Dr. King answered. "How much?"

"Fifteen," the driver told him, and Dr. King paid the fare.[179]

This was the first day of bus integration in Montgomery and the official end of the bus boycott that had lasted for more than a year. After Rosa Parks was arrested for violating segregation laws 381 days earlier, Black residents vowed to stop riding the city bus until they were treated equally to their White counterparts.[180] Black residents made between thirty thousand and forty thousand daily rides, which was reduced to between three hundred and four hundred after one year of the boycott. This had cost the city $750,000 in lost revenue.[181] Not surprisingly, the boycott was deemed "undemocratic" and said to be surely initiated by people who wanted to cause racial tension.[182]

Dr. King and Reverend Abernathy may have gone down in the pages of history as heroes of the civil rights movement, but there were thousands of men and women whose names we will never know who sustained the boycott during its darkest days. Determined citizens walked hundreds of miles through the streets of Montgomery instead of riding the bus. And behind it all were the women who kept everyone fed. It's likely that on the day Dr. King and Reverend Abernathy took their famous bus ride, the two men ate lunch in Georgia Gilmore's kitchen.

Georgia Gilmore was born in 1920, the year that Alabama turned 101 years old.[183] The state had seen a lot of changes during its first century. If Anne Royall had shown up for a visit in the year that Georgia was born, she would not have recognized her beloved vacation spot. Her carriage from 1819 would have been able to travel down a paved road, the colonel's wife would have legally been allowed to vote, and, thanks to Prohibition, everyone who followed the law would have been sober. All of this was a far cry from the Alabama of Anne's time, where everyone started the day with a shot of whiskey and men were expected to drink as much liquor as possible at political functions.

When the civil rights era came to Alabama, Georgia was a widow with six children. She worked as a midwife and cooked in a segregated restaurant called the National Lunch Company. When she left work to deliver babies, one of her children grabbed her place on the line. After her picture was posted on the front page of the *Chicago Defender* for her involvement in the boycott, she was fired. Dr. King encouraged her to start working for herself rather than get another job and even gave her the money to start cooking at home. What began as a catering and lunch delivery service turned into a secret lunchroom where everyone met to talk. Pretty soon, Georgia was feeding the resistance—the people fighting for the right to ride the bus with the same dignity as the other half of Montgomery's population.[184]

Georgia's kitchen was not segregated, and she fed anyone who showed up at her door. Black and White residents ate together in a way that could not have been done in a regular restaurant. It was not just Dr. King and Reverend Abernathy, but Lyndon B. Johnson and Robert F. Kennedy also ate in her kitchen. Blue-collar workers, maids, and even Aretha Franklin dined with Georgia. John Kennedy requested her food while he was visiting Maxwell Air Force Base, and Georgia cooked potato pies and chitterlings (fried pig intestines) for the president of the United States. She did talk to his brother Edward when he came by her kitchen. Both Catholics, she felt a good connection to Edward Kennedy. Her kitchen was a safe space, with delicious food and Georgia's big personality. "I just served 'em and let 'em talk," Georgia said in a 1978 interview.[185]

She cooked the kind of foods that fill you up and make you happy, including pork chops, fried chicken, potato salad, macaroni and cheese, fried fish, coleslaw, and collard greens. She made the best kind of southern desserts, the kind I ate when I visited friends who had mothers from Alabama. When your own mother has never heard of 7-Up cake, you learn to love it on a much deeper and more spiritual level than your friends who take it for granted. Pound cake, peach cobbler, pineapple upside-down cake—all of those delicious, rich desserts that just fill you up with love and happiness are what Georgia made for the resistance. It's not hard to see why she was so loved.

She was not just beloved; she was also a woman to be feared if you hurt someone she loved. Georgia was fiercely protective not just of her own family but of her community. When a storeowner refused to sell her grandson a loaf of bread, she went down to the store and beat the man with his own gun. "Don't mess with

Georgia Gilmore seated in the audience at Holt Street Baptist Church. *Courtesy of the Alabama Department of Archives and History.*

Georgia Gilmore; she might cut you," Thomas Jordan, the pastor of the Lilly Baptist Church, said of her.[186] A fierce but adorable woman who could cook really good food was just what the movement needed.

"Georgia's food was cooked on the mama level, and Georgia was like Big Mama—the southern-type big mamas—she took on the personality of ten or fifteen of them," Reverend Al Dixon said of Georgia.[187] She also had a playful spirit that put people at ease and made them feel like they belonged. She could cook, but it was not just her cooking that drew people in, it was Georgia herself, who made people feel loved as well as fed. "Come here, little heifer, and get your dinner," Georgia would say to Dr. King. Yes, the dignified hero of the civil rights movement was a "heifer" in her kitchen, just like everyone else—unless she called them a whore. Governor George Wallace was not a whore or a heifer—just Guvs.[188] It's possibly for the best that John F. Kennedy never made it to her kitchen. Calling the president of the United States a heifer might not have gone over well.

She wasn't just everyone's mama who fried chicken and baked pound cakes. Georgia organized other cooks like herself, and together, they cooked and sold cakes and fried chicken and other kinds of delicious goodies to raise money for the boycott. They were known as the Club from Nowhere because, "Where did the money come from? Nowhere." That way, nobody could be fired the way Georgia had been fired from the National Lunch Company. Georgia was the only one who knew all of the names of the ladies who cooked and also of the people who bought the food. The money raised by the club helped pay for alternate transportation and other expenses.[189] Without Georgia and her fried chicken, the Montgomery bus boycott may not have ever succeeded. The following recipe was given to the Kitchen Sisters by Mark Gilmore, Georgia's son, and published in their book *Hidden Kitchens* (2005).

Georgia Gilmore's Homemade Pound Cake

1 pound butter
2 cups sugar
6 eggs
1 teaspoon vanilla
a little milk
2 cups flour

First, blend the butter and sugar together in a large bowl. Then add the eggs, vanilla, and milk. Add the flour and blend together. Lightly grease a tube pan. Pour in the batter and bake at 350°F for 1 hour. Turn it upside sown—let it cool and then cut it.[190]

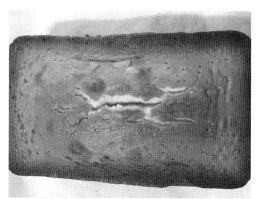 

Georgia Gilmore's poundcake made with all-purpose flour. Self-rising flour is recommended and will give you a much fluffier cake. *Author's collection.*

Mary baked this poundcake for me in June 2021, the last of the recipes prepared in this book. Tonight, as I type these words, my husband is finishing off the cake. It was a very good cake, but it's extremely rich. A little goes a very long way. I also recommend covering it in heaps of whipped cream. I know that's not part of the recipe, but it's very yummy. Georgia knew what she was doing.

Lannie's Bar-B-Q Spot
2115 Minter Avenue
Selma, Alabama 36703

Since 1942, Lannie's Bar-B-Q has been serving up delicious plates of barbecue to the people of Selma. From the very beginning, Lannie's was a family business. Lannie's husband slaughtered the hogs himself after her twelve-year-old daughter carried them home from the stockyard in the basket of her bicycle. After boiling off all the hair and butchering the hogs on the table, they smoked the pork in their own pits.[191]

For more than seventy years, Lannie's has remained a family business. Each new generation grows up learning how to work in the restaurant and take pride in what their family has accomplished. Although some things have remained the same, like their pulled pork sandwiches with the signature crackling on top, the family has adjusted to the changing times. The original dirt floor is long gone, and they no longer slaughter their own pigs. The Lannie's menu has also expanded beyond barbeque to include burgers, chicken wings, and other tasty goodies.[192]

Like Georgia Gilmore's kitchen in Montgomery, both Black and White residents ate together at Lannie's, violating segregation laws. In an interview with Jim Shahin for the *Washington Post*, Lannie's granddaughter Deborah Hatcher remembered the Ku Klux Klan from her childhood. "Lights flashing. Horns blasting. We would go in the house and turn the lights out. This was a mean, cruel place back in those days."[193] When civil rights activists came to Selma, Lannie's brought them food. During the meetings at the Brown Chapel AME that were held to organize the famous march from Selma to Montgomery in 1965, the family once again supplied the movement with barbecue.[194]

Today, you can still eat the original pulled pork sandwich that made them famous, but you can also get some fried okra or onion rings on the side. You will be eating the same foods that sustained the civil rights activists during the 1960s, and you can say hello to the descendants of the chefs who fed them.

Brenda's Bar-B-Que Pit
1457 Mobile Road
Montgomery, Alabama 36108

James and Jereline Bethune originally opened a nightclub called the Siesta Club in 1944, which also sold food. The couple soon decided they would prefer to sell barbecue, so they changed the name to Brenda's, in honor of their second daughter. Soon afterward, James died, and Jereline ran the restaurant alone during the segregation era. In an interview in 2015, Jereline's granddaughter explained how much trouble a Black woman went through with official inspections. "She would do everything that was asked, and then she would come in and be asked to do something else."[195]

Today, the carry-out restaurant remains a family business, which is how Jereline envisioned it. She wanted it to be a legacy for the family for generations, and that's what it is. Her son and granddaughter serve up chicken, pork, fish, and sweet potato pie. They also sell the fan-favorite dishes of ribs and pig ear sandwiches.[196] It's a carry-out restaurant only, but dining in has not been necessary to keep Brenda's a popular spot for almost eighty years.

During the civil rights era, Brenda has helped spread the word about the NAACP meetings. This was during the time before printers were a common household item, and the Ku Klux Klan still had a foothold in the area.[197] Today, you can taste the same foods that were popular during the civil rights era and say hello to the descendants of the people who helped the movement.

Chris' Hot Dogs
138 Dexter Avenue
Montgomery, Alabama 36104

Chris Katechis opened his hot dog restaurant more than one hundred years ago, and it has been one of Montgomery's most popular spots ever since. The special sauce for the hot dogs took Chris a few years to master, but once the customers told him he had hit the perfect recipe, it was never changed.[198]

Chris was popular with everyone, and his restaurant served all classes of customers. His clientele included Governor George Wallace, who was a regular patron before he became governor. In an interview with WSFA News, Chris's son Theo explained that, in those early days, Wallace did not always have enough money to pay for hot dogs, so Chris sold to him on credit. During his run for governor, Wallace returned the favor with the largest order the restaurant has ever had: three thousand hot dogs.[199] Wallace was hardly the only celebrity to eat at Chris's Hot Dogs. Hank Williams had his own booth, where, after ordering a shot and a beer, he would sit and write his songs. President Franklin Roosevelt also ate Chris's hot dog, although his was delivered to him.[200]

During the civil rights era the restaurant also fed Martin Luther King Jr. and Rosa Parks, who usually came in for a hot dog after getting off the city bus. Just like Lannie's and Brenda's, Chris's felt the presence of the Ku Klux Klan. Even though his restaurant was segregated, he allowed Black customers to come in through the front door. The restaurant received threats over this, which shows just how powerful the KKK's presence was at the time.[201] When Chris promoted a Black employee to cashier, the KKK threatened to burn down the restaurant. Chris had no choice but to find the employee another job.[202]

Just like Lannie's and Brenda's, Chris's is a family business. Theo runs the business with his son Gus, as Chris died in 1988. The original lunch counter is still there. It's a counter that was once segregated, but now, everyone eats together. As Theo says, that's "the way it should be."[203]

In the End

For this chapter, I had to abandon my rule of only using historic structures that had not been built as restaurants but serve food today. They may exist, but I could not find any. This is a shame. This is an era to be celebrated with poundcake and sweet tea. Martin Luther King Jr., Rosa Parks, and, of course, Georgia Gilmore are important parts of the history of Alabama. The era of civil rights is a serious topic, but it should be celebrated for the incredible people who made it what it was.

The history of Alabama is made up of many different parts. It's Anne Royall and her broken-down carriages and her milk punch. It's Nicey Pugh and the ripe peach she plucked from the tree. It's James Williams and his venison. It's even William Howard Russell and his opossum dinner. Some of our history is ugly. Some of it is beautiful. But all of it is ours, and all of it can be tasted for what it is—even if it's only a fragment.

EVEN MORE HISTORICAL SPOTS TO GRAB A BITE

Writing this book during the pandemic meant that I did not get to travel across the state, visiting historical sites and eating local food as I had originally planned. I did manage to travel to a few locations, but there is so much more to see and eat. Below is my list of places I want to visit, and I'm sure it's not even close to a complete list of what Alabama has to offer. I called or stopped by each location to make sure they would be accessible to readers. If a location was not available to talk with me, they were not included in this list. This also means that these places will be expecting to see you. If I missed anything, be sure to let me know. You can find me driving around Alabama, looking for history, and, of course, eating good food. See you out there.

Smith-Byrd House (Built in the mid-1880s)
137 North Washington Street
Prattville, Alabama 36067
Autauga County

334-365-1459

The Smith family built the house and remained there for more than seventy years. Today, you can enjoy an afternoon tea Wednesday through Saturday from 10:00 a.m. to 4:00 p.m. Call for reservations.

Jesse's Restaurant (Built in 1921)
14770 Oak Street
Magnolia Springs, Alabama 36555
Baldwin County

251-965-3827

Originally built as the Moore Brothers General Store in 1921, today, it's a restaurant open for lunch and dinner every day except Sunday. One of the dining rooms is the original Magnolia Post Office built in the 1950s. Reservations are highly recommended. Call for more information.

The Copper Kettle Tea Bar (Built circa 1900)
106 North Chicago Street
Foley, Alabama 36535
Baldwin County

251-609-2832

This is the last surviving building on Chicago Street from the early 1900s. Today, the Copper Kettle Tea Bar serves an assortment of teas and treats, but in the 1930s, it was used to house railroad workers.

Stacey's Olde Tyme Soda Fountain (Built in 1927)
121 West Laurel Avenue
Foley, Alabama 36535
Baldwin County

251-943-7191

Since 1927, Stacey's Drugstore has been selling old-fashioned ice cream treats, including egg creams and phosphate sodas. You can still buy a cup of coffee for its original selling price of ten cents, but Stacey's is famous for its key lime milkshake. Although it was built as a pharmacy, it closed that part of its business in February 2020, and now, it just focuses on treats.

Classic on Noble (Built in 1894)
1024 Noble Street
Anniston, Alabama 36201
Calhoun County

256-237-5388

Built in 1894 as the Levy-Clark Saloon, it was converted into a fine-dining restaurant in the 1990s. It is closed on Mondays. Call for more information. You will most likely get the answering machine, but they are very good at returning calls.

St. James Hotel Selma (Built in 1837)
1200 Water Avenue
Selma, Alabama 36703
Dallas County

334-553-6700

The hotel was built in 1837 but was closed for many years. It was just recently opened again, and today, visitors can eat in the place where wealthy planters ate before the Civil War and where Jesse James hung out while on the lookout for the police. Jesse liked the third floor because it had a good view of the street below. The hotel was once put on the "Ghost Trail," as it was reported that the outlaw's ghost was still hanging out at the hotel.[204] Perhaps he was still looking out for the police in the afterlife.

St. James Hotel in the 1930s. Selma, Alabama. *Courtesy of the Library of Congress.*

Mama Misitano's Café
(Built in 1979 in the Sand Mountain Shooting Club)
626 Bloodworth Road
Boaz, Alabama 35956
Etowah County

256-593-8027

Originally built as a gun repair shop in 1979, it soon added a small sandwich bar and a shooting range. Today, they have added three paintball fields, and the tiny sandwich bar became a café that serves homemade Italian dishes made from recipes that were brought over in the 1900s. Owners Dan and Jan have been married for fifty-three years, and they are both descended from Italian immigrants. The recipes come from Dan's grandparents, who arrived in Alabama as teenagers in the early 1900s. Dan is pure southern and might talk your ear off, and if Jan has time, she might ask you to move over while you're eating and have a seat at your table. They view everyone who comes in as "adopted family," and this makes sense, as Grandma Jan and Grandpa Dan; their two sons; and their grandchildren are their only employees. The family makes their own pizza crust and bakes their own bread, and everything else is made from scratch. The restaurant is open Tuesday through Sunday, but Sundays are done differently, as everything is served family style. Call for more details, but do not call on Monday. The shooting range is reserved only for prescreened clients.

Payne's Soda Fountain (Built in 1869)
101 East Laurel Street
Scottsboro, Alabama 35768
Jackson County

256-574-2140

In 1899, William Henry Payne established the W.H. Payne Drug Company in the Jackson County Courthouse Square. Today, the building is still there and is still run by the Payne family. William's granddaughter occasionally pops in to see how the business is running, which is the oldest soda fountain in Alabama. They stopped dispensing medicines in the early 1990s, but the soda fountain has kept a few early prescriptions and other reminders of its origins. Today, they sell old-fashioned ice creams, sodas, malts, and sandwiches.

Rx Lounge
Hotel Indigo Birmingham Five Points S–UAB (Built in the 1930s)
1023 Twentieth Street South
Birmingham, Alabama 35205
Jefferson County

205-933-9555

This Art Deco building from the 1930s was constructed to be used as a medical office. It was converted into a hotel in the 1980s, but they have kept the medical essence from the building's original purpose. The personnel at the front desk wear scrubs and sport an assortment of test tubes and Erlenmeyer flasks. The Rx Lounge will serve "prescriptions" of food and drinks every evening except Sundays. Call for details.

Arlington Antebellum Home and Garden (Built circa 1850)
331 Cotton Avenue Southwest
Birmingham, Alabama 35211
Jefferson County

205-780-5656

This mansion was built by Judge William Mudd in 1850. Every Thursday in June, July, and August, the public is invited to have lunch at the mansion. Seating begins at 11:30 a.m. and ends at 1:00 p.m. Each week, the menu is different. The cost is twenty dollars per person, which includes admission into the house museum. Reservations are required. Lunch is also served on the second Thursdays of September and November. Reservations are required. These were the prices at the time of this writing—please call to make sure prices or times have not changed.

Main Street Café (Built in 1955)
101 Main Street
Madison, Alabama 35758
Madison County

256-461-8096

Built in 1955 as a city hall, the building served different municipal functions until the 1970s. It was converted into a café in 2000, and the original bars and cinder blocks from the old jail cells were incorporated into the café. For over twenty years, the lunch menu has not changed, as Madison locals expect traditional southern food. For dinner, there is an entirely different menu, which is less traditional and more fine dining. The café is closed on Sundays. Call for more information.

Burritt on the Mountain (Built circa 1938)
3101 Burritt Drive Southeast
Huntsville, Alabama 35801
Madison County

256-536-2882

Dr. William Henry Burritt built his mansion in 1938. Today, this is a museum and historic park that sit on 167 acres. They seem to have a little bit of everything, including a few special dining events. Most importantly, every Wednesday, from 5:00 p.m. to 8:00 p.m., April through October, they offer Cocktails on the View. Enjoy snacks and cocktails while you watch the sun go down.

Harrison Brothers Hardware (Built in 1897)
124 Southside Square
Huntsville, Alabama 35801
Madison County

256-536-3631

Brothers James and Daniel Harrison opened a hardware store in 1897. The name has been kept, along with the original counters, shelves, and fixtures, but

Interior of Harrison Brothers Hardware. Huntsville, Alabama. *Courtesy of the Library of Congress.*

hardware is no longer sold here. The only items that were sold by James and Daniel that can still be purchased today are marbles. You can buy jams, jellies, relishes, and Alabama-made D.P.'s Pool Hall Slaw. Other goodies include locally made pickled peaches, pickled honey cinnamon beets, and pickled smokin' okra. When you buy one of these gourmet pickles made by a local artisan, they will be rung up for you on the original cash register from 1907.

Battle House Hotel (Built in 1908)
Official name: The Battle House Renaissance Mobile Hotel & Spa
26 North Royal Street
Mobile, Alabama 36602
Mobile County

251-338-2000

There has been a hotel on this site for two hundred years, although the current hotel was built in 1908. The Battle House offers a variety of dining options, but I do recommend breakfast. I had a working breakfast there years ago, and

Daily menu from the Battle House Hotel in Mobile, Alabama, 1857. *Courtesy of the Rare Book Division, New York Public Library, Digital Collections.*

I have always regretted not going back with more time to properly enjoy it. When you walk into the hotel, the grandeur can be a little overwhelming. Give yourself a minute to take it all in before sitting down to eat.

Firehouse Wine Bar (Built in 1806)
216 St. Francis Street
Mobile, Alabama 36607
Mobile County

This building was constructed in 1806 and was incorporated as a Hook and Ladder Firehouse in the 1840s. In the early 1900s, Mobile started using engines instead of horses to carry water, and the building was too narrow to accommodate the new technology. Today, it is a bar with some intriguing appetizers. They also offer special events with wine or food themes. Call for details.

Visitation Monastery (Built in 1855)
2300 Spring Hill Avenue
Mobile, Alabama 36607
Mobile County

251-473-2321

This is a monastery on beautiful, quiet grounds set back from a very busy street. There is a gift shop as well, which sells candy made by the nuns, who have been cooking there since 1957. This monastery is very close to the

Convent of Visitation. Mobile, Alabama, c1906. *Courtesy of the Library of Congress.*

Bragg-Mitchell Mansion, and both buildings went up around the same time. Although this list was intended to include locations I have not visited yet, I cheated on this one. Mary and her entire family were quarantined due to a coronavirus exposure, so I bought heavenly hash for both of us. Between my husband and me, our entire box was gone by the time the night was over. Sadly, they do not sell divinity.

Freight House (Built in 1915)
200 Railroad Street Southwest
Hartselle, Alabama 35640
Morgan County

256-773-4600

Built in 1915 by the South & North Alabama Railroad, the building was soon used by the Louisville & Nashville Railroad as a loading depot. Thousands of bales of cotton were shipped from this depot, making it an important transportation hub for the area. Local residents also used it to ship smaller packages, which made it an important site for socializing. Today, the Freight House still has the original steel beams, brick, concrete, and wooden scale, which, over the years, weighed thousands of pounds of cotton. It's now the place to go for steak, and the restaurant specializes in Hereford beef. They prefer to think of their chefs as "good southern cooks" who serve up homemade pimento cheese and crab cakes, along with steaks and chicken. They also offer nine-inch, four-layer cakes for dessert in strawberry, Italian cream, and coconut flavors, and for the kids, there is a build-a-train cookie. The trains still roll by, but they no longer stop at the depot. Call for more details.

Red's Little Schoolhouse (Built in 1910)
20 Gardner Road
Grady, Alabama
Montgomery County

334-584-7955

This is a former schoolhouse from 1910 that was converted into a restaurant in 1985. They sell country food with a buffet. The owner of the restaurant bakes fourteen pies before 9:30 a.m. every morning, and sometimes, they make more in the afternoons. Most everything is homemade, including all the salad dressings (except for the low-calorie dressing, because as she told me, "I don't know how to make that"). The restaurant is a little bit out of the way, which hasn't stopped anyone from finding her. "If I cook, they'll come." The schoolhouse is open from Wednesday to Sunday; it's closed Mondays and Tuesdays. Call for more details.

NOTES

Introduction

1. Weymouth T. Jordan, "Early Ante-Bellum Marion, Alabama: A Black Belt Town," *Alabama Historical Quarterly* 5 (1943): 21.
2. "Wm. Barron's House Warming," *Marion Times Standard*, April 23, 1909.
3. Ibid
4. Ladies of the St. Francis Street Methodist Episcopal Church, Mobile, Alabama, *Cookbook*, 203.
5. "House Warming," *Marion Times Standard*.

Chapter 1

6. Edge, *Potlikker Papers*, 215–20.
7. Yoni Appelbaum, "Making Bread Great Again," *Atlantic*, June 29, 2016, www.theatlantic.com.
8. John Kessler, "Scott Peacock Is Back in the Kitchen," *Garden & Gun*, April/May 2019, www.gardenandgun.com.
9. For further reading on Beard, Child and Claiborne, consult Kamp, *United States of Arugula*.
10. McNamee, *Man Who Changed*.
11. Wallach, *How America Eats*, 13, 15, 37, 46.

12. Thomas Jones Taylor, "Early History of Madison County: And Incidentally of North Alabama," *Alabama Historical Quarterly* 1 (Spring 1930): 153–54.
13. Brown and Akens, *Alabama Heritage*, 68–70.

Chapter 2

14. Royall and Griffith, *Letters from Alabama*, 32–33.
15. Katherine Abernathy, "Anne Royall," Encyclopedia of Alabama, www.encyclopediaofalabama.org.
16. Royall and Griffith, *Letters from Alabama*, 38–43.
17. Ibid., 118–38.
18. Ibid., 179–83.
19. Johnson, *Alabama Barbeque*, 28–31.
20. Benton, *Very Worst Road*, 57–67.
21. Ibid., 53–56.
22. Ibid., 71–75.
23. Ibid., 80.
24. Ebenezer Hearn, "The Autobiography of Ebenezer Hearn," Montgomery, AL: Alabama Department of Archives and History, 1–7.
25. Kathryn Braund, "Creek War of 1813–14," Encyclopedia of Alabama, January 30, 2017. www.encyclopediaofalabama.org.
26. Hearn, "Autobiography," 1–7.
27. Ibid.
28. Joshua Shiver, "Gaines Ridge Dinner Club," Encyclopedia of Alabama, January 24, 2020, www.encyclopediaofalabama.org.

Chapter 3

29. Kuh, *Finding the Flavors*, 209.
30. Hymenean, *Tuscumbian*, January 24, 1825.
31. Marilyn Jones Carter, "State Restores Lovely Home," *Anniston Star*, May 27, 1990.
32. Alabama Historical Commission, "Belle Mont Mansion," Encyclopedia of Alabama, December 4, 2018, www.encyclopediaofalabama.org.
33. "Obituary," *Tuscumbian*, December 13, 1825.
34. Alabama Historical Commission, "Belle Mont Mansion."

35. Ibid.

36. Sarah Woolfolk Wiggins, "John Gayle," Encyclopedia of Alabama, May 22, 2018, www.encyclopediaofalabama.org.

37. The following section is taken mostly from Gayle, Wiggins and Truss, *Journal of Sarah Haynsworth Gayle*.

38. Yerby, *History of Greensboro*, 29–30.

39. Wiggins, "John Gayle."

40. Gayle, Wiggins and Truss, *Journal of Sarah Haynsworth Gayle*, 214–19.

41. Ibid.

42. Van Buren Brugiere, *Good-Living*, 509–10.

43. Elizabeth Fox-Genovese discusses in detail Sarah's conflicting ideas about slavery and love here (*Plantation Household*, 22–28).

44. Kolchin, *American Slavery*, 141.

45. Gayle, Wiggins and Truss, *Journal of Sarah Haynsworth Gayle*, 285–87.

46. Fox-Genovese, *Plantation Household*, 27–28.

47. Gayle, Wiggins and Truss, *Journal of Sarah Haynsworth Gayle*, 280.

48. Kolchin, *American Slavery*, 153.

49. Unless otherwise noted, all of the information in this section came from two sources: "Narrative of James Williams, an American Slave, Who Was for Several Years a Driver on a Cotton Plantation in Alabama: Electronic Edition," Documenting the American South, a project sponsored by University Library of the University of North Carolina at Chapel Hill, and Carrie Spell, "Narrative of James Williams," Encyclopedia of Alabama, January 26, 2016, www.encyclopediaofalabama.org.

50. Kolchin, *American Slavery*, 125–26, 166.

51. Oakes, *Slavery and Freedom*, 21.

Chapter 4

52. Thwaite, *Glimpses*, 85.

53. Gary R. Mullen, "Philip Henry Gosse," Encyclopedia of Alabama, December 19, 2017, www.encyclopediaofalabama.org.

54. Thwaite, *Glimpses*, 177–79; Information about Jeanne Villepreux-Power, the woman who invented the aquarium, can be found here: Marissa Fessenden, "A 19th Century Shipwreck Might Be Why This Famous Female Naturalist Faded to Obscurity," *Smithsonian Magazine*, June 2, 2015, www.smithsonianmag.com.

55. Thwaite, *Glimpses*, 29, 79.

56. Most of the material here comes from this journal, which Gosse published as a book: Gosse and Jackson, *Letters from Alabama.*
57. Mullen, "Gosse"; Gosse's drawings from 1838 can be viewed here: Auburn University Digital Libraries, "P.H Gosse Digital Collection," diglib.auburn.edu.
58. Gosse and Jackson, *Letters from Alabama*, 117.
59. Ibid., 59–60, 105, 141–42.
60. Ibid., 41, 143, 288, 234–35.
61. Ibid., 226–34.
62. Ibid., 250.
63. Ibid., 196.
64. Ibid., 45.
65. Ibid., 250–55, 278.
66. Thwaite, *Glimpses*, 94–95; Mullen, "Gosse."
67. Gosse and Jackson, *Letters from Alabama*, 45–47. The original entry is much longer and has been edited by the author for clarity.
68. PBS, "The Works Progress Administration," www.pbs.org; Library of Congress, "Born in Slavery: Slave Narratives from the Federal Writers' Project, 1936 to 1938," www.loc.gov.
69. All of Nicey's information comes from Ila Prine's documentation (Ila B. Prine, "Aunt Nicey Pugh: Slave Narratives from the Federal Writers' Project, Vol. 1, Alabama, Aarons-Young," www.loc.gov).
70. Ila B. Prine, "A Slave Is Given His Young Missy's Name: Slave Narratives from the Federal Writers' Project, Vol. 1, Alabama, Aarons-Young," www.loc.gov.
71. Ila B. Prine, "He Misses Dem Set-Down Hawgs: Slave Narratives from the Federal Writers' Project, Vol. 1, Alabama, Aarons-Young," www.loc.gov.
72. Alabama Historical Commission, "History of Gaineswood," www.ahc.alabama.gov.
73. Eleanor Evins Stewart, "Gaineswood: Home of General Nathan B. Whitfield," in National League of American Pen Women, *Historic Homes.*
74. Hale, "Gaineswood," in *Historic Plantations*, 66–69.
75. Whitfield, "Crumpets," in *From Gaineswood*, 19.
76. For more information on Christmas on the River, check out the Demopolis website: www.christmasontheriverdemopolis.com.

Chapter 5

77. Cooper and Terrill, *American South*, 383–84.

78. Crawford and Russell, *Russell's Civil War*, xvii–xxi.

79. Briggs, *Victorian People*, 61.

80. Roy Greenslade, "Drama in Crimea—Historic Dispatches from the Father of War Reporting," *Guardian*, July 28, 2014, www.theguardian.com.

81. Crawford and Russell, *Russell's Civil War*, xxv.

82. Russell, *My Diary*, 230–38.

83. Ibid., 238, 244.

84. Ibid., 244–45.

85. Russell, *Pictures*, 18.

86. Russell, *My Diary*, 249–50.

87. Ibid., 237.

88. Owens, *Owens' New Cook Book*, 143.

89. Hague and Fox-Genovese, *Blockaded Family*, 1–6.

90. Bunn, *Civil War*, 19, 62–64.

91. Hague and Fox-Genovese, *Blockaded Family*, 16.

92. Ibid., 13–14.

93. Ibid., xxiii–xxv.

94. Ibid., 13, 15; Bunn, *Civil War*, 12.

95. Hague and Fox-Genovese, *Blockaded Family*, 101–2.

96. "Substitute for Coffee," *Tuscaloosa Weekly Times*, August 28, 1861.

97. "How to Get the Very Best of Coffee at about Ten Cents Per Pound," *Alabama Beacon*, November 22, 1861.

98. "For the *Southwestern Baptist*," *Southwestern Baptist*, December 12, 1861.

99. Willis Likes, "Notebook Belonging to Willis Likes, Containing Information About Plantation and Domestic Life from About 1810 to 1866," Lela Legare Papers, Alabama Department of Archives and History.

100. Hague and Fox-Genovese, *Blockaded Family*, 102.

101. Ibid., 31–32, 47, 102.

102. Ibid., 46–47.

103. Mahan, *Admiral Farragut*, 288.

104. Jennifer M. Murray, "Battle of Mobile Bay," Encyclopedia of Alabama, www.encyclopediaofalabama.org.

105. Delaney, *Craighead's Mobile*, 172–73.

106. Ibid.

107. Monica Tapper, "Bragg-Mitchell Mansion," Encyclopedia of Alabama, www.encyclopediaofalabama.org.

108. Ibid.

Chapter 6

109. Fox-Genovese, *Plantation Household*, 196–97.

110. Lorraine Boissoneault, "The Political Cartoon That Explains the Battle Over Reconstruction," *Smithsonian Magazine*, March 2, 2107, www.smithsonianmag.com.

111. T.A. Frail, "The Trial of the Century That Wasn't," *Smithsonian Magazine*, May 2017, www.smithsonianmag.com.

112. "The Martyr of Fort Monroe, *American Citizen*, July 11, 1866.

113. Norrell, *Up from History*, 23.

114. F. Erik Brooks, "Booker T. Washington," Encyclopedia of Alabama, www.encyclopediaofalabama.org.

115. Washington, *Slavery*, 5, 9.

116. Ibid., 6–7.

117. Ibid., 24–46.

118. Ibid., 53, 58.

119. Ibid., 74.

120. Norrell, *Up from History*, 42–44, 52–54.

121. Washington, *Slavery*, 111–14.

122. Ibid.

123. Norrell, *Up from History*, 62–69.

124. Robert J. Norrell, "The Uplift of Humanity: Booker T. Washington in Context," *Alabama Heritage*, Spring 2011.

125. Hamilton and Matte, *Seeing Historic Alabama*, 17–18; Author's phone call with Lyla Peebles.

126. Women's Guild, "Mooresville Walking Tour," Huntsville Museum of Art, 1975, www.hsvmuseum.com, 12–13.

127. Author's phone call with Lyla Peebles.

128. "Memories—From the Land of Used-To-Be," *Shelby County Reporter*, March 20, 1952.

129. "Funeral Held Tuesday for Former Resident," *Shelby County Reporter*, March 6, 1947.

130. "Church Entertainment: Nice Sum Realized by Columbiana Presbyterian Women," *Montgomery Advertiser*, May 5, 1907.

131. "Good Form and Entertainment," *Harper's Bazar*, October 1908, 1,038.

132. Elizabeth Talbott, "Giving a Shadow Party," *Table Talk* 42, no. 11 (n.d.): 30–33.

Chapter 7

133. Henley, *This Is Birmingham*, 31–32.

134. Ibid., 41, 49.

135. Jessie C. Bonner, "The Calico Ball," in Pioneers Club, *Early Days*, 99–102.

136. Birmingham Public Library, "Birmingham's Population, 1880–2000," www.bplonline.org.

137. Birmingham City Council, "About Birmingham," www.birminghamal.gov.

138. Monica Tapper, "Frank P. O'Brien," Encyclopedia of Alabama, www.encyclopediaofalabama.org.

139. Ibid.

140. Monica Tapper, "Bossie O'Brien Hundley Baer," Encyclopedia of Alabama, www.encyclopediaofalabama.org.

141. Ibid.

142. Thomas, *New Woman in Alabama*, 161.

143. Bossie O'Brien Hundley Baer, *With the Passing Years*, (N.p.: n.p., n.d.), 102.

144. Ibid.

145. Ibid.

146. "Suffrage Tea—Today at Southern Club," *Birmingham News*, May 5, 1914.

147. Burr, *Woman Suffrage Cookbook*, 101.

148. "Wise-Merritt Wedding Occurs," *Montgomery Advertiser*, December 2, 1915.

149. "Theater Man Shot to Death in Birmingham," *Anniston Star*, July 1, 1947.

150. "Death Scene Is Described by Neighbor," *Birmingham News*, July 1, 1947.

151. "Baffled Officers Re-Grill Negroes in Merritt Slaying," *Birmingham News*, July 2, 1947.

152. "If Barks Were Words, Cookie Could Answer," *Birmingham News*, July 2, 1947.

153. "Negro Confesses to Pistol Slaying of Theater Man," *Birmingham News*, July 4, 1947.

154. "Lie Detector Inconclusive in Merritt Murder—Coroner," *Birmingham News*, July 1, 1947.

155. "Negro Confesses," *Birmingham News*.

156. "Simmons Tells of Two Officers Who Beat Him," *Birmingham News*, October 22, 1947.

157. Don F. Wasson, "Alabama Board Grants 3 Pardons, 28 Paroles," *Montgomery Advertiser*, July 19, 1969.

158. "Saturday to Sec Redmont Opening," *Birmingham News*, May 7, 1925.

159. "Redmont Hotel," *Birmingham News*, November 9, 1935.

160. "Redmont Hotel Thanksgiving Dinner," *Birmingham News*, November 27, 1935.

161. "Rainbow Room at Redmont, City's Newest Dining Place, Ready to Open," *Birmingham News*, October 13, 1937.

162. Irene S. Levine, "A Swedish Smorgasbord Done Right," *Chicago Tribune*, March 21, 2014.

163. Author's phone call with Taylor Padlan, May 12, 2021.

Chapter 8

164. Sulzby, *Alabama Hotels*, 135–44.

165. Augustine Meaher, "Point Clear Marine Training Command," Encyclopedia of Alabama, www.encyclopediaofalabama.org.

166. Edwina Parker, "Old Fashioned Christmas Drinks," *Table Talk* 22, no. 12 (December 1907): 467.

167. Most of the information in this section came from Wade Hall's book, but the author also spoke with Kenny's son Tony May and Clyde's sister Zelda. They are proud of their family legacy and were very helpful in the author's understanding of the lives of both Clyde and Kenny (Hall, *Waters of Life*, 39, 16, 14).

168. Hall, *Waters of Life*, 13, 48–49.

169. Ibid., 25–27.

170. Ibid., 27–28, 31–32, 37.

171. Ibid., 36.

172. Beth Greenfield, "Concerts by (and for) Singers," *New York Times*, April 20, 2007, www.nytimes.com; Melissa Block, "Preserving the Sacred Harp Singing Tradition," NPR, December 5, 2003, www.npr.org.

173. Hall, *Waters of Life*, 36–37.

174. Ibid., 50–53, 60.

175. Ibid., 54–62.

176. Ibid., 61–62.

177. Ibid., 47.

178. Monica Tapper, "Clyde May," Encyclopedia of Alabama, www.encyclopediaofalabama.org.

Chapter 9

179. "Boycott Leaders Take Desegregated Bus Ride," *Alabama Journal*, December 21, 1956.

180. "Capital Fears Trouble in Negro Bus Dispute," *Anniston Star*, December 5, 1955.

181. "Montgomery Bus Boycott Controversy Is Now One Year Old," *Opelika Daily News*, December 6, 1956.

182. "Two Wrongs," *Montgomery Advertiser*, December 2, 1956.

183. Emily Blejwas, "Georgia Gilmore," Encyclopedia of Alabama, September 24, 2019.

184. Silva and Nelson, *Hidden Kitchens*, 196–99.

185. Lenore Reese, "King Helped Put Local Woman in Lunch Business," *Alabama Journal*, April 4, 1978.

186. Edge, *Potlikker Papers*, 22.

187. Silva and Nelson, *Hidden Kitchens*, 195.

188. Ibid.

189. Edge, *Potlikker Papers*, 17–18.

190. Silva and Nelson, *Hidden Kitchens*, 207.

191. Meredith Bethune, "A Lifetime of Barbeque in Selma," *Gravy* (Fall 2016), www.southernfoodways.org.

192. Johnson, *Alabama Barbeque*, 74–76.

193. Jim Shahin, "They Fed the Civil Rights Movement. Now Are Black-Owned Barbecue Joints Dying?" *Washington Post*, February 22, 2016.

194. Johnson, *Irresistible History*, 76.

195. Matt Okarmus, "Brenda's Barbeque Is Family Tradition," *Montgomery Advertiser*, September 7, 2015.

196. Ibid.

197. Johnson, *Irresistible History*, 72.

198. WSFA 12 News, "Iconic Montgomery," March 25, 2015.

199. Ibid.

200. Elisabeth Sherman, "In Montgomery, the Memory of the Civil Rights Movement Lives on in the Kitchen," *Food & Wine*, February 26, 2018, www.foodandwine.com.

201. WSFA 12 News, "Iconic Montgomery."

202. Sherman, "In Montgomery."

203. WSFA 12 News, "Iconic Montgomery Restaurant Had Front-Row Seat to Civil Rights Movement," March 25, 2015.

Chapter 10

204. "Ghost Trail May Scare Up Tourism Dollars," *Macon Telegraph*, July 10, 2009.

BIBLIOGRAPHY

Books

Benton, Jeffrey C. *Through Others' Eyes: Published Accounts of Antebellum Montgomery, Alabama*. Montgomery, AL: NewSouth Books, 2014.

———. *The Very Worst Road: Travelers' Accounts of Crossing Alabama's Old Creek Indian Territory, 1820–1847*. Tuscaloosa: University of Alabama Press, 2009.

Briggs, Asa. *Victorian People: A Reassessment of Persons and Themes, 1851–1867*. Chicago: University of Chicago Press, 1975.

Brown, Virginia Pounds, and Helen Morgan Akens. *Alabama Heritage*. Huntsville, AL: Strode Publishers, 1967.

Bunn, Mike. *Civil War: Eufaula*. Charleston, SC: The History Press, 2013.

Burr, Hattie A. *The Woman Suffrage Cookbook*. Boston: Hattie A Burr, 1886.

Cooper, William J., Jr., and Thomas E. Terrill. *The American South: A History*. Vol. 2. Lanham, MD: Rowman & Littlefield Publishers, 2009.

Crawford, Martin, and William Howard Russell. *William Howard Russell's Civil War: Private Diaries and Letters, 1861–1862*. Athens: University of Georgia Press, 1992.

Delaney, Caldwell. *Craighead's Mobile*. Mobile, AL: Haunted Bookshop, 1968.

Edge, John T. *The Potlikker Papers: A Food History of the Modern South*. New York: Random House, 2018.

Fox-Genovese, Elizabeth. *Within the Plantation Household: Black and White Women of the Old South*. Chapel Hill: University of North Carolina Press, 1988.

Gayle, Sarah Ann Haynesworth, Sarah Woolfolk Wiggins, and Ruth Smith Truss. *The Journal of Sarah Haynsworth Gayle, 1827–1835: A Substitute for Social Intercourse*. Tuscaloosa: University of Alabama Press, 2013.

Gosse, Philip Henry, and Harvey H. Jackson. *Letters from Alabama, (U.S.): Chiefly Relating to Natural History (Library of Alabama Classics)*. Tuscaloosa: University of Alabama Press, 1993.

Hague, Parthenia, and Elizabeth Fox-Genovese. *A Blockaded Family: Life in Southern Alabama During the Civil War*. Lincoln: University of Nebraska Press, 1991.

Hale, Jennifer. *Historic Plantations of Alabama's Black Belt*. Charleston, SC: The History Press, 2009.

Hall, Wade. *Waters of Life from Conecuh Ridge: The Clyde May Story*. Montgomery, AL: New South Books, 2007.

Hamilton, Virginia Van der Veer, and Jacqueline Anderson Matte. *Seeing Historic Alabama: Fifteen Guided Tours*. Tuscaloosa: University of Alabama Press, 1996.

Henley, John C. *This Is Birmingham: The Founding and Growth of an American City*. Birmingham, AL: Southern University Press, 1969.

Johnson, Mark R. *An Irresistible History of Alabama Barbeque: From Wood Pit to White Sauce*. Charleston, SC: The History Press, 2017.

Kamp, David. *The United States of Arugula*. New York: Broadway Books, 2006.

Kolchin, Peter. *American Slavery, 1619–1877*. New York: Hill and Wang, 2003.

Kuh, Patric. *Finding the Flavors We Lost*. New York: HarperCollins Publishers, 2016.

Ladies of the St. Francis Street Methodist Episcopal Church, Mobile, Alabama. *Gulf City Cookbook*. Dayton, OH: United Brethren Publishing House, 1878.

Mahan, A.T. *Admiral Farragut*. New York: D. Appleton and Company, 1893.

Martin, Gay N. *Alabama's Historic Restaurants and Their Recipes*. Winston-Salem, NC: John F. Blair, 1998.

McNamee, Thomas. *The Man Who Changed the Way We Eat: Craig Claiborne and the American Food Renaissance*. New York: Simon and Schuster, 2012.

National League of American Pen Women. *Historic Homes of Alabama and Their Traditions*. Reprint, Birmingham, AL: Southern University Press, 1969.

Norrell, Robert J. *Up from History: The Life of Booker T. Washington*. Cambridge: Cambridge University Press, 2011.

Oakes, James. *Slavery and Freedom: An Interpretation of the Old South*. New York: W.W. Norton & Company Inc., 1990.

Owens, Frances E. *Mrs. Owens' New Cook Book and Complete Household Manual*. Chicago: Owens Publishing Company, 1899.

Pioneers Club. *Early Days in Birmingham*. Birmingham, AL: Southern University Press, 1968.

Royall, Anne Newport, and Lucille Griffith. *Letters from Alabama, 1817–1822*. Tuscaloosa: University of Alabama Press, 1969.

Russell, William Howard. *My Diary North and South*. Vol. 1. London: Bradbury and Evans, 1863.

———. *Pictures of Southern Life*. New York: James G. Gregory, 1861.

Silva, Nikki, and Davia Nelson. *Hidden Kitchens*. Danvers, MA: Rodale Books, 2005.

Sulzby, James Frederick. *Historic Alabama Hotels and Resorts*. Tuscaloosa: University of Alabama Press, 1989.

Thomas, Mary Martha. *New Woman in Alabama: Social Reforms and Suffrage,1890–1920*. Tuscaloosa: University of Alabama Press, 1992.

Thwaite, Ann. *Glimpses of the Wonderful: The Life of Philip Henry Gosse*. London: Faber & Faber, 2002.

Van Buren Brugiere, Sara. *Good-Living: A Practical Cookery-Book for Town and Country*. New York: G.P. Putnam's Sons, 1890.

Wallach, Jennifer Jensen. *How America Eats: A Social History of U.S. Food and Culture*. Lanham, MD: Rowman & Littlefield Publishers, 2012.

Washington, Booker T. *Up from Slavery*. Cambridge, MA: Riverside Press, 1901.

Whitfield, Mary Augusta. *From Gaineswood and Other Whitfield Kitchens*. Dauphin Island, AL: A Little Publishing House Inc., 1977.

Williamson, Joel. *A Rage for Order: Black-White Relations in the American South Since Emancipation*. New York: Oxford University Press, 1986.

Yerby, William Edward Wadsworth. *History of Greensboro, Alabama from Its Earliest Settlement*. Montgomery, AL: Paragon Press, 1908.

Magazines, Newspapers and Others

Alabama Beacon
Alabama Heritage
Alabama Historical Quarterly
Alabama Journal
American Citizen
Anniston Star
Atlantic, www.TheAtlantic.com

Birmingham News
Chicago Tribune
Food & Wine
Garden & Gun, www.GardenandGun.com
Guardian, www.TheGuardian.com
Harper's Bazar
Macon Telegraph
Marion Times Standard
Montgomery Advertiser
New York Times, www.nytimes.com
NPR, www.npr.org
Opelika Daily News
PBS, www.pbs.com
Shelby County Reporter
Smithsonian Magazine, www.Smithsonianmag.com
Southwestern Baptist
Table Talk
Tuscaloosa Weekly Times
Tuscumbian
Washington Post
WSFA News 12

Interviews

Diane Moore
Lyla Peebles
Melinda Farr Brown
Michael Herzog
Mitchell Brown
Susan Stein
Taylor Padlan
Tony May

Websites

Alabama Department of Archives and History
www.archives.alabama.gov

Alabama Historical Commission
www.ahc.alabama.gov

Birmingham City Council
www.birminghamal.gov

Birmingham Public Library
www.bplonline.org

Christmas on the River
www.christmasontheriverdemopolis.com

Documenting the American South
www.docsouth.unc.edu

Encyclopedia of Alabama
www.encyclopediaofalabama.org

Library of Congress
www.loc.gov

Southern Foodways Alliance
www.southernfoodways.org

ABOUT THE AUTHOR

M onica Tapper is a historian from Alabama. She holds
a master's degree in history with a concentration in
public history. She is interested in the intersection
where food and history meet.